INSIGHT

Mallorca

Discovery
CHANNEL

APA PUBLICATIONS
Part of the Langenscheidt Publishing Group

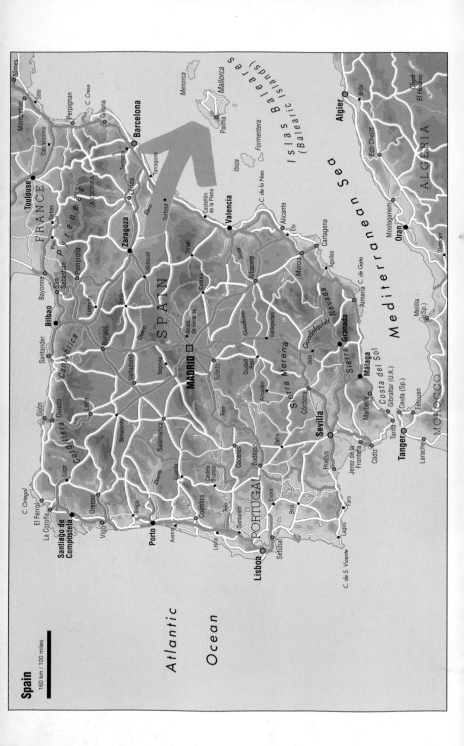

Spain

160 km / 100 miles

Welcome

This guidebook combines the interests and enthusiasms of two of the world's best-known information providers: Insight Guides, who have set the standard for visual travel guides since 1970, and Discovery Channel, the world's premier source of non-fiction television programming.

Its principal aim is to help visitors with limited time get the most out of Mallorca with the aid of 17 carefully designed itineraries put together by Insight Guides' correspondents on the island, Don Murray and Ana Pascual. The tours venture off the beaten track as much as possible (though they include the best of what the 'beaten track' has to offer as well) to discover the essential flavour of Mallorca – from the lively and attractive city of Palma to the island's most picturesque mountain villages, its most dramatic views, its most interesting architecture, its tranquil hilltop hermitages and the best of its many superb beaches. In addition to the tours, there are sections on history and culture, shopping, eating out, nightlife, sporting facilities, family leisure activities and a calendar of special events. A detailed practical information section at the back of the guide covers transport, money matters, communications, etc., and includes a list of recommended hotels.

Don Murray and **Ana Pascual** have lived on Mallorca for many years, dividing their time between sailing and writing. Between them, they have written more than a dozen books and several hundred articles on the island. Their chief advice to visitors is to leave their car as often as possible and enjoy the island on foot, leaving plenty of time for long, lazy lunches and soaking up the sun.

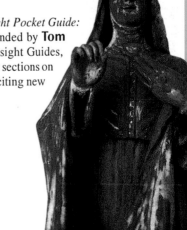

Subsequent editions of *Insight Pocket Guide: Mallorca* have been updated and expanded by **Tom Le Bas** and **Pam Barrett**, editors at Insight Guides, who road-tested the tours and added new sections on sports, leisure activities and Palma's exciting new galleries, hotels and restaurants.

HISTORY AND CULTURE

From the civilising influences of the Romans and the Moors to the effects of modern tourism – an account of the people and issues that have shaped Mallorca **11**

ITINERARIES

These 17 carefully planned routes concentrate on Mallorca's principal sights and beauty spots, as well as venturing off the beaten track into the lesser known interior of the island.

Pages 2–3: terraced fields near Banyalbufar
Pages 8–9: on the beach at Port d'Alcúdia

History & *Culture*

The formation of the Balearic islands began when sediments accumulated in the primordial seas over 100 million years ago. This limestone bedrock was forced upwards by tectonic forces to create a peninsula jutting out to sea from the present-day Spanish coast around Valencia. A subsequent rise in sea levels broke up the peninsula into the separate islands.

Mallorca can be divided into three geographical areas: the craggy mountains of the Serra de Tramuntana, running along the northwest coast from Andratx to the Formentor peninsula; the lower, rounded hills of the Serres de Llevante parallel to the eastern coast; and the central plain *(pla)*, a mostly flat area punctuated by occasional wooded hills.

The indigenous Mallorcan vegetation, *garigue,* is typical of the Mediterranean – scrub forests of pine, holm oak, wild olive, lentiscus and dwarf fan palms – which is still found in uncultivated areas of the island away from the mountains. At higher elevations is the *maquis,* comprising rosemary, myrtle and lavender.

The relatively few mammal species include pine martens and mountain goats. Birds, on the other hand, have always been plentiful. Even though their habitat is under constant threat, counting the migrators and a few indigenous species, they number today well over 2,000 species.

Rainfall on the island is mostly slight (though heavier in the mountains), and generally falls between October and April. Summers are hot, sunny and almost completely dry.

Crossroads of the Western Mediterranean

Mallorca, like other major islands of the Mediterranean, has attracted a cornucopia of conquerors, invaders and settlers. Archaeological evidence suggests that neolithic pastoralists arrived on the Balearic Islands from mainland Europe sometime around 5000BC. These early settlers found shelter in natural caves, but later began to construct larger cave complexes in the limestone found across much of the archipelago. Following the arrival of a race of settlers known as the Beaker People around 1500BC, metallurgical skills were developed, and the first open-air settlements constructed.

Many stone and earth settlements were established at this time; most of these were dominated by a distinctive cone-shaped watchtower, or *talaiot,* of which there are numerous remains across the island – best preserved at Capocorb Vell and Ses Païsses *(see pages 56 and 64).*

The Balearics' location on the great trading routes that crisscrossed the Mediterranean Sea brought a great deal of contact with the ancient world. Eivissa (Ibiza) became an important commercial centre for the Phoenicians, and, later on, Carthaginian

Left: the Talayotic settlement at Capocorb Vell
Right: *hondero* (stone slinger) at S'Hort del Rei garden in Palma

traders. The Phoenicians established a trading post near present-day Alcúdia, although Mallorca was likely to have been of only minor significance to them. There are references in classical texts to Mallorcan *honderos* (stone slingers) fighting for the Carthaginians in the Punic Wars (the Greeks named the islands the Balearics, after *ballein* – which means to throw from a sling).

Despite the efforts of the sling-shots, the Romans eventually defeated the Carthaginians to become the major power in the western Mediterranean. They soon decided to put a stop to the piracy that was rife in the Balearics, and organised an expedition to conquer and settle Mallorca. In 123BC Quinto Cecilio Metelo conquered the island, and for five and a half centuries it was subject to the vicissitudes of Roman history. Historians believe that at the time there were two major centres, Pollentia (beside Alcúdia) and Palma. After a few more centuries of 'ups and downs' under the successive domination of the Vandals and the Byzantines, the Muslims began 200 years of attacks on the island at the beginning of the 8th century AD. In 902 the entire archipelago was annexed to the Emirate of Córdoba.

While Roman culture probably had the greatest impact on Mallorcan social patterns, the influence of the Moors was responsible for important advances in the island's agriculture, along with development of the island's crafts and commerce. It is also easy to pinpoint the Moorish contribution to the island's folklore, language and cuisine.

Jaume I, the Conqueror

It was the Mallorcan Moors' plundering of Catalan boats that finally provoked the powerful, newly-united kingdom of Catalunya and Aragón to plan the overthrow of the island. In the autumn of 1229, 15,000 men with 1,500 horses aboard 155 ships set sail from Salou, in Tarragona. Bloody details aside, King Jaume I of Aragón, the Conqueror, annexed the island after a three-month siege of the city of Medina Mayurka (Palma). On his death in 1276, the monarch subdivided this enlarged kingdom between his two sons – the younger, Jaume, got Mallorca, which now became independent. His elder son, Pedro, inherited Aragón and Catalunya, but was infuriated by Mallorca's independence. Pedro's son, Alfonso III, invaded Mallorca in 1285, but after his death in 1291 Jaume II was restored to the throne.

The island lived through what the historians call a 'Golden Age' from 1276 to 1344. Jaume II's reign saw a flowering of the island's agriculture, industry and maritime trade. New villages were founded, coins minted, and work begun on an enormous cathedral on the site of the city's main mosque. Various other impressive buildings were constructed in the years that followed, including Bellver Castle and the Convent of Sant Francesc, while the Moors' Almudaina was transformed into a splendid Gothic palace. In fact, almost all traces of the Muslim period were destroyed in the wake of the Christian conquest. This was also the time of the Mallorcan philosopher, scientist and Christian missionary, Ramón Llull.

Above: monument to Ramón Llull (1235–1316), Mallorcan scholar and missionary

The Balearics continued to enjoy prosperous independence until relations with the Kingdom of Aragón deteriorated, a situation which culminated in Pedro IV's invasion in 1344. Now tied to the mainland, a long period of economic downturn began. This fall from grace was later exacerbated by the decline of Mediterranean trading routes following the fall of Constantinople in 1453 and the discovery of a new sea route to the Orient around the Cape of Good Hope. In 1479 the Balearics were united with the Kingdom of Spain as part of the political union of Castile and Aragón, which relegated the islands' status still further – to the central government they were little more than a far-flung provincial backwater; this was compounded by the discovery of America, as Spain turned its back on the Mediterranean and looked west to the riches of the New World.

A series of uprisings in the 15th and 16th centuries were caused by economic difficulties and popular discontent against the nobility, many of whom had neglected their estates – becoming absentee landlords after union with Spain led them to spend more and more time on the mainland. Periodic persecution of the islands' Jewish inhabitants also occurred under the guise of the Inquisition. Meanwhile, plague was rampaging through Europe, drastically reducing populations, and soon arrived on the island, killing thousands.

The War of the Spanish Succession

Until the crisis engendered by the lack of an heir to the Spanish throne at the end of the 17th century, Mallorca had enjoyed a state of semi-autonomy. The islanders were opposed to the possibility of a French Bourbon king acceding, with ideas of an 'absolute' monarchy, and instead backed the Austrian pretender to the throne, Charles.

Above: jousting Moors and Christians
Right: a 17th-century Mallorcan knight

Yet Felipe de Bourbon (Felipe V) finally prevailed, and in 1715 his troops arrived on Mallorca. The island lost its title of kingdom as The Grand and General Council was replaced by an 'Audience' supervised by a Captain General of the King's troops, and the use of Castilian (the Spanish language) was made obligatory for all public and official transactions.

Mallorca lived in constant fear of pirate attacks from North Africa – this explains why many Mallorcan towns are located a few kilometres inland, with a smaller port settlement nearby (examples are Sóller, Pollença and Andratx). In response to this persistent threat, several generations of notable Mallorcan sailors were given permission by the king to 'defend' their homeland. Needless to say, the licence – the *patente de corso* – proved enormously beneficial. The most famous of the corsairs (named after this licence) was Captain Antoni Barceló, who eventually achieved the rank of Lieutenant General of the Spanish Armada by such acts as renting ships to the navy whenever it was short of sea power.

Another famous personage from this era was the Mallorcan missionary Fray Junípero Serra *(see pages 48–9)*. Born in the inland village of Petra, Serra travelled considerably further than Barceló. Without the Mallorcan missionary, San Francisco and many other Californian cities might not exist today.

Catalan Refugees

The Napoleonic wars, at the beginning of the 19th century, brought Catalan refugees pouring into Mallorca, with both social and economic unrest in their wake. The islands were poor and many people, seeing the writing on the wall (and the lack of food in the pantry) emigrated to the mainland, Algeria and the New World. Things improved towards the end of the century as communications with the mainland were established, shipping lines were set up to exploit trade with the Indies, the marshy plain near Palma was pumped dry and the land reclaimed for agricultural purposes. The railway was built and a timid regionalism emerged with the renewed use of the Catalan language.

But the end of the century saw another falling of local economic fortunes. *Phylloxera* ruined the island's booming wine business; and the loss of Cuba,

Puerto Rico and the Philippines as colonies put an abrupt halt to much local shipbuilding.

The first half of the 20th century on Mallorca was dominated by two men: the politician Antoni Maura and the financier Joan March. Maura, the leader of the Conservative Party, spent all his political life in Madrid, but never lost the loyal support of his fellow islanders. The life of Joan March Ordinas was the archetypal 'from rags to riches' story. Born in a Mallorcan village at a time of strong class prejudices, he became not only the richest man in Spain, but was thought to be the third richest man in the world (after John Paul Getty and Howard Hughes). The March Foundation is extremely influential in supporting the arts today *(see pages 24 and 28)*.

The Mallorcans continued into the third decade of the 20th century much as they had left the 1800s – provincial, extremely religious and politically conservative. With the governing classes firmly on the side of Francisco Franco from the very beginning, the islands saw little violence during the Spanish Civil War. During the dictatorship, the political situation in the islands was similar to that on the peninsula. It wasn't until the 1960s and the arrival of mass tourism that Mallorca began to dismantle its traditional way of life. In 1975, with the death of Franco, the island began the work of recovering its cultural identity. In 1978, under the Statute of Autonomy, the Balearic Islands, like a number of other regions, were given a degree of autonomy and became an autonomous province five years later.

The Language Issue

When Mallorca became an autonomous region, Mallorquí, the local version of Catalan, was recognised officially as the language of the island. Many people felt very strongly about it, and discouraged the use of Castilian. Others were prepared to let the two languages exist side-by-side. With the passage of time, most islanders are more relaxed about the language question. Catalan/Mallorquí is now taught in schools, and most people speak both Mallorquí and Spanish (Castilian). A new language issue is excercising people's minds these days. Of the six million plus tourists who visit Mallorca every year, quite a few are seduced by the island's natural beauty, mild climate and pleasant lifestyle, and decide to stay. Entire villages are taken over by German and British ex-pats, and many signs are in their languages. The Balearic Government has responded by passing a law stipulating that all signs should first be in Catalan or Spanish, and only then in a foreign language.

Left: Palma's waterfront in the mid-17th century
Above: the new constitution of 1978 gave the Balearics a measure of autonomy

Mallorcans are deeply divided over what to do about the exploitation of the island itself. They are polarised between maintaining the incredible pace of growth that Mallorca has enjoyed over the past 25 years, or facing the reality that times are changing and the goose that laid the golden egg may not go on laying. The big money is on continuing growth, while ecologists are on the other side, trying hard to protect the island's natural beauty and resources. May people who were enticed to Mallorca are realising that parts of 'La Isla de la Calma' are turning into a jungle of noise and concrete. By the late 1990s, a new emphasis on quality and on safeguarding the environment had begun to take root; building restrictions were implemented and certain areas were declared protected zones. Some of the worst hotel complexes have even been torn down, although some mass-market resorts in the south are beyond repair.

In May 2002 an 'eco-tax' came into effect – a small per capita tax on hotel guests, the revenue from which was to improve the Balearic Islands' ecology and help fund urban restoration. However, after much wrangling about its possible deleterious effects on tourism, and a shift to the right in island politics, the tax was discontinued at the end of 2003.

A Tradition of Hospitality

Being islanders, the Mallorcans have withstood a long history of invasions by nearly everyone who could reach their coastline. As a result, they have become defensive and nationalistic. But they have also learned the advantages of trade. They have learned to accommodate their 'visitors' while accommodating themselves. Mallorcans are an extremely friendly and sociable people. They are quite happy to chat with a stranger in a bar, and will greet everyone upon entering and bid everyone goodbye when

they leave. They are answered by a chorus of *'Bon dia!'* from everyone within range. Most Mallorcans seem genuinely pleased if a foreigner speaks to them in either of their two languages. A tradition of hospitality has developed from centuries of subjection to all kinds of invaders and, now, to tourists. But the Mallorcans expect something in return for this hospitality. They want to make a living.

Where is Mallorca going from here? Almost everyone agrees that growth cannot continue at its present accelerated rate, and the current objective is to take tourism further upmarket, with an emphasis on *agroturisme* (rural tourism), offering accommodation in farm houses and country retreats, and encouraging visitors to enjoy the natural beauties Mallorca still has to offer.

Left: stopping for a chat

HISTORY HIGHLIGHTS

1300–1000 BC: Talayotic period.

123 BC: The Balearics absorbed into the Roman Empire.

2nd century AD: Christianity established.

707: First Muslim attack.

902: Annexation to the Emirate of Córdoba.

1015: Mallorca is annexed to another Muslim 'kingdom', the 'Taifa of Denia'.

1087–1114: Mallorca becomes an independent *taifa*.

1114: A group of Pisa-Catalans conquer Eivissa and Mallorca; siege of Palma lasts eight months; after the city is sacked, the invaders go home.

1115–1203: The Almorávides, a tribe from North Africa, arrive to help the Mallorcan Muslims and stay on to occupy the island, which experiences a period of prosperity.

1203–29: Political instability and aggression under the Almohadian Muslims encourages the newly united Catalans and Aragónese to invade.

1229: King Jaume I of Aragón occupies and conquers Mallorca on 31 December, after three months of fighting. Period of prosperity and building ensues – work is begun on Palma cathedral.

1235–1315: Life of Mallorcan philosopher and scientist, Ramón Llull.

1276: Death of Jaume I and creation of the independent Kingdom of Mallorca ruled by Jaume II.

1285: First attempt by the Catalans to recover the Kingdom of Mallorca by force. Later expedition returned by order of the Pope.

1312–24: Reign of King Sanç, son of Jaume II of Mallorca.

1324–44: Reign of King Jaume III of Mallorca, bringing economic prosperity. Palma is one of the richest cities in the Mediterranean.

1344: Troops of Pedro IV of Aragón invade and reincorporate the islands into the Kingdom of Aragón.

1479: Kingdom of España formed by uniting the kingdoms of Castille and Aragón, including Mallorca. Economic decline begins.

1700: Felipe de Bourbón ascends to the throne. Beginning of the War of Spanish Succession.

1713–84: Life of Fray Junípero Serra, founder of the missions of California.

1785: Treaty of Algiers signed, ending piracy while establishing the Mallorcan 'corsairs'.

1808–13: The War of Independence against Napoleon. Refugees arrive on Mallorca, provoking social tension.

1820–22: Massive emigration to Algeria and South America.

1837: First regular steamship line between Mallorca and the mainland.

1879–98: The years of the 'gold fever'. Period of prosperity thanks to the wine and almond trades. Ends with arrival of the *phylloxera* epidemic and loss of Spain's last colonies.

1936–9: Spanish Civil War.

1939–75: Dictatorship of Franco.

1960s: Mass tourism brings prosperity, but great environmental damage.

1978: Approval of new Spanish Constitution, which opens the doorway to the creation of autonomous regions.

1983: Approval of the Statutes of Autonomy for the Balearics; first elections held shortly thereafter.

1986: Spain joins the European Union.

1990s–present: The Balearics enjoy the highest per capita income in Spain.

2002 Euro becomes official currency.

2002 PSOE (Socialist Party) comes to power in March elections in Spain, but the Partido Popular is dominant in the Balearic Island government.

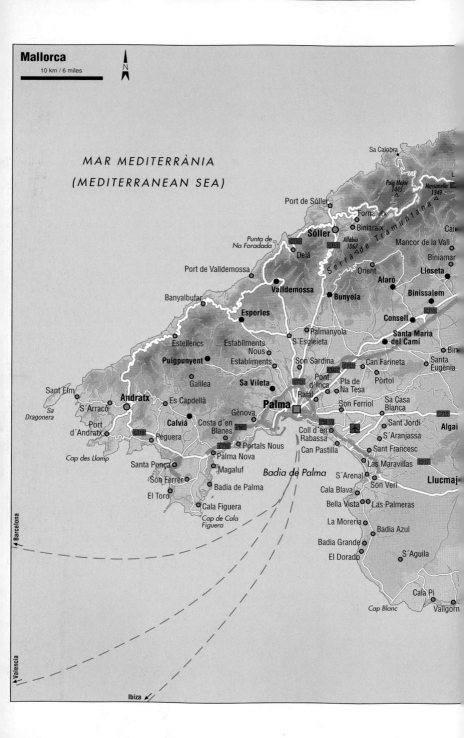

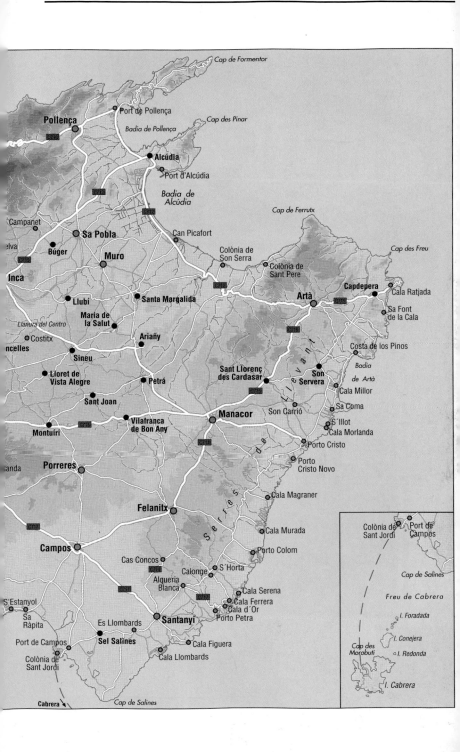

Mallorca
itineraries

1. PALMA HISTORICA *(see map, p22)*

A guided walking tour combining modern art, ancient cloisters, great museums, hot chocolate in an 18th-century café, a walk among the flower sellers, a *llagosta* in Bar Bosch, ancient shipyards and a king's garden.

Palma is an attractive city, and its compact centre is ideal for a walking tour. This itinerary guides you to the best of the city's art and architecture, both ecclesiastical and secular and describes the major museums. A second route *(pages 29–30)* visits some great attractions to the west of the city.

Start at the **Parc del Mar**, a landscaped area, with an artificial lake, which lies between the city walls and the busy main road that parallels the bay. The park is home to a collection of modern sculptures as well as a colourful mural by Joan Miró. From here you get an excellent view of the cathedral and the restored 17th- and 18th-century **city walls**, which more or less follow earlier defences dating back to Arabic times.

Enter the old city (Casc Antic) through the walls by way of the **Porta de la Portella**, to the east of the cathedral. Immediately on the left is the late 17th-century **Ca la Torre**, now the Collegi d'Arquitectes. Next door is the baroque doorway of the **Posada de Cartoixa**, and at the first corner, **Can Formiguera**'s 17th-century façade and balcony.

A Moorish Relic

Straight ahead, Carrer de la Portella takes you to the **Museu de Mallorca** (open Jun–Oct: Tues–Sat 10am–2pm, 5–7pm; Nov–May: 9.30am–1.30pm, 4–6pm, Sun 10am–2pm; entrance fee), housed in the splenddi **Ca La Gran Cristiana**. As well as Roman remains, Gothic and Islamic art, and some 20th-century paintings, it has an excellent section dedicated to a little-known Mallorcan ceramic factory, La Roqueta.

On parallel Carrer Serra are the **Banys Arabs** (Arab Baths; open Apr–Sept: daily 9.30am–8pm; Oct–Mar: 9.30am–6pm; entrance fee). Set in a peaceful garden, the baths date back to the times of the Walis (Arab governors) during the 9th and 10th centuries, and are among the few surviving Moorish structures in Mallorca. The first, circular room, with a cupola and skylights, housed the hot bath whose waters were warmed by Roman-style underfloor heating; the second room has a barrel vault. The capitals on the supporting columns are of varying styles, which reflects the Moors' practice of re-using materials from demolished buildings.

At the next corner take a hard right and follow this short street till it enters the patio of the **Convent of Santa Clara**, founded by King Jaume I in 1256. The church was built in the 1600s. Turn

Left: *Moderniste* flair at the Forn des Teatre *pastelaria*
Right: city wall watchtower

back onto Carrer de Santa Clara, and then right at Carrer de Monti-Sión. At No 6 is **Can Malonda**, also dating from the 17th century, and further along the baroque façade of the church of **Monti-Sión**. If you go further along the street, then take a right turn into Carrer Calders, you will come to the the **Museu Diocesà** (open Mon–Sat 10am–1pm, 4.30–7pm; entrance fee). Its true home is in the Palau Episcopal, but this is closed for lengthy renovation work. The museum contains Mallorcan religious art from Roman times to the 19th century.

Go down narrow Carrer de la Criança and follow it to the end before turning left on Carrer del Sol. The city's most important Renaissance façade, that of the **Casa del Marquès del Palmer**, is at No 7. Turn right onto Pare Nadal and then right again into the Plaça de Sant Francesc. Immediately to your right is the 18th-century **Can Moragues**, with a wonderful courtyard. Palma has many such Renaissance mansions, built after the fire that destroyed much of the medieval city; one of the delights of walking around the old city is to peer

through the wrought-iron gates into the beautiful courtyards *(patios)*. In summer there are guided tours of the city's patios, when you can actually go inside (tel: 971 711 547 or go to the Visitors' Centre at Carrer Sant Roc; tours in English usually on Tuesday and Thursday).

On the opposite side of the square, to the right of the church, is the entry to the cloister of the **Basílica de Sant Francesc** (open Mon–Sat 9.30am–noon, 3.30–6pm, Sun 9.30am–noon; free). Built by the Franciscans in the 13th century, it embodies architectural elements added throughout the 16th century. The church, a Gothic structure with a baroque façade, may be entered from from the lovely cloister; the dark interior houses the tomb of the philosopher and missionary Ramón Llull (1235–1316). Outside the main doorway is a statue of Mallorcan missionary Fray Junípero Serra, founder of the Californian missions *(see page 48)*, with an Amerindian convert at his side.

Baroque Highlights

From the church, turn left onto Carrer de Savellá. At No 6, **Can Vivot** has one of the city's most important courtyards, in the baroque style, dating from the early 18th century. It is still home to the Count and Countess of Savellá. Opposite, at No 13, look into the restored 17th-century baroque entrance of **Can Savellá**.

One block to the right, on Carrer Sanç, is the oldest café in the city, founded in 1700, the attractive, tiled **Can Joan de S'Aigo**. Specialising in Mallorcan hot chocolate, wonderful almond ice cream and typical Mallorcan pastries, it used to be Joan Miró's favourite café.

Return to the end of the street, turn left and continue to **Plaça de Santa Eulàlia** with a Gothic church of the same name, dating from the 14th century. Leaving the square on Carrer Morey, you will find **Can Olesa** at No 9; it has one of the finest examples of Palma's courtyards, dotted with glossy potted plants. The façade is 16th-century Renaissance. At the next corner turn right onto Carrer de Sant Pere Nolasc, which runs along the front of the gardens of the Bishop's Palace, then turn right onto Carrer de Zanglada.

Where the street ends at Carrer de l'Almudaina, look right. The **Arc de l'Almudaina** is generally thought to be Arabic, but some experts believe it dates back to Roman times. Continuing left along the same street, both the Gothic 13th-century **Can Bordils** (No 9) and its 17th-century neighbour, **Can Oms** (No 7a) are interesting public buildings that may be entered during office hours. On Carrer Palau Reial, to the right, the ochre colonnades of the **Parlament de les Illes Baleares** (Island Parliament) run almost to **Plaça Cort**, the hub of city life since the 13th century. The present

Above Left: Junípero Serra statue at Sant Francesc
Right: City Hall façade on Plaça Cort

Ajuntament (Town Hall) has an overhanging roof, supported by carved beams. You may enter the street level hallway, where you will see an elegant imperial staircase and a pair of ceremonial Mallorcan *gigants* of papier-mâché. Plaça Cort's other dominant feature is a gnarled and ancient olive tree in the centre.

North from the Plaça Cort

On the corner of Carrer Santo Domingo is **Can Casellas**, a stunning example of Modernist architecture. From Plaça Cort, continue north along Carrer Colòm; at the far end on the left are two further examples of *Modernisme*: grabbing most of the attention is the colourfully tiled **Can Rei** with its grotesque frowning window box, while next door stands the eclectic work of

local architect Gaspar Bennàssar, **Almacenes Aguila**. Both buildings date from the early years of the 20th century.

The archways lead into the spacious **Plaça Major**. Built at the beginning of the 19th century on the site of the Inquisition building, it is surrounded by attractive yellow façades with dark green shutters, and the tables of several cafés. On Monday, Friday and Saturday morning it is the site of a good crafts market, and most days there are street entertainers and musicians here. Straight through the square, on Carrer Sant Miquel, you will find, in a striking building on the left, at No 11, the **Museu d'Art Espanyol Contemporani** (open Mon–Fri 10am–6.30pm, Sat 10am–1.30pm; entrance fee), displaying works by Picasso, Miró, Dalí and Juan Gris, among others. The collection belongs to the March Foundation, a philanthropic institution set up in 1955 by local financier Joan March – who at one time was reputed to be the third richest man in the world.

Further along on the same side is the ancient church of **Sant Miquel**, where the first mass after the Christian reconquest was celebrated. On the other side are the church and cloister of **Sant Antoniet**. Built in the 18th century in late baroque style, the church is now deconsecrated and used as an exhibition space for installation art and other displays.

Continuing along the increasingly downbeat Carrer Sant Miquel, pass the church of **Santa Catalina**, turn right and enter busy **Plaça d'Espanya**. In the centre is a monument to 'Jaume I, Conqueridor de Mallorca'. Other notable structures are the eclectic buildings of the railway station on the far side of the heavy traffic of **Avinguda Joan March Ordinas**; and the two corner buildings, which also display eclectic Modernist touches.

Go down Carrer d'es Oms, turning left onto **La Rambla**. This tree-lined

Above: La Rambla, the flower sellers' street. **Above Right:** at the Bar Bosch
Right: Gaudí's influence is obvious on the Can Casayas building, Plaça del Mercat

avenue, which is properly known as Via Roma, was, until the 17th century, the watercourse through Palma. Walking down the central promenade among the flower stalls you may catch sight, on the right-hand side, of a beautifully restored rose-coloured façade. The brace of Roman centurions at the end of the avenue date from the Franco era.

Follow the road round to the right; on the left is the Classicist façade of the **Teatre Principal**, which has been undergoing renovations for a number of years. Across the street, the restored **Gran Hotel**, a magnificent art nouveau structure built in 1902 by Catalan architect Lluís Domènech i Montaner, is now a cultural centre run by the **Fundació La Caixa** (open Tues–Sat 10am–9pm, Sun 10am–2pm; free), which has a good bookshop and a smart café as well as large exhibition spaces and a permanent display of work by Hermen Anglada Camarasa (1872–1959), who lived in Pollença. Directly opposite is the *Moderniste* frontage of the Forn des Teatre bakery, and further along you pass the **Palau de Justicia**, in a seignorial house dating from the 18th century. Next door sit the delightful twin *Moderniste* buildings that comprise **Can Casayas**. Further along on the right-hand side, the attractive 18th-century **Círculo de Bellas Artes**, regularly houses exhibitions.

Continue west along the busy Carrer Unió and stop for coffee at the **Bar Bosch**, in Plaça Rei Joan Carles I, which also serves its own variety of sandwiches in rolls called *llagostas* (lobsters). From the bar's outside tables you can see a central fountain, its obelisk supported by stone turtles. Heading off to the west is the broad Avinguda Jaume III, Palma's main shopping street, but our route goes left, towards the cathedral and the sea.

Ancient Streets

Follow the **Passeig des Born**, the wide, tree-lined promenade, guarded at either end by stone sphinxes. Originally a long finger-like inlet leading from the sea, it was filled in the 17th century, in order to provide an arena in which popular festivals could be held, including jousting. To the right stands the elegant arched loggia of the 18th-century **Palau Sollerich** (open Tues–Sat

10am–2pm, 5–9pm, Sun 10am–1.30pm; entrance fee for some exhibitions). The building, which is owned by the town hall, holds regular art exhibitions and houses a café and bookshop. A little farther down, turn right into Carrer Sant Feliu. The narrow streets of this ancient corner of the city, known as the **Puig de Sant Pere** and extending west from Es Born to the Passeig de Mallorca, are home to some of its most lively bars and restaurants, especially around Carrer Apuntadors and Plaça de Sa Llotja. Several interesting art galleries and specialist shops are also tucked away in the back streets.

Turn left into Carrer Montenegro. On the right-hand side is the baroque façade of **Can Montenegro**, which belonged to one of the most powerful families in the city. The large plaque on the front refers to a member of the family who was Grand Master of the Order of Malta. Turning right into Carrer Glória and continuing to the end, you will find yourself between two particularly interesting houses. On the left is the enormous **Cal Capitá Flexes**, which was

Top: the spacious interior of Sa Llotja is used for temporary art exhibitions
Above: modern art in the gardens of S'Hort del Rei

built by a wealthy corsair – or pirate – in the 17th century. In front, and on the opposite side of Glória, is a patio opening to **Can Llull**, a tasteful restoration of an 18th-century house.

Statues and Sculptures

Descending a slight hill you arrive at **Plaça de la Drassana**, a pleasant neighbourhood square that was the site of Mallorca's most important shipyard from the 13th to the beginning of the 19th century. In the centre is a statue of a renowned Mallorcan sailor, Jaime Ferrer. Leaving the square by Carrer Consulat, you see **Can Chacón** above to the right; to the left is the **Consulat del Mar**, built in the 17th century as a maritime court. A cannon and a large anchor stand outside the building.

Turning left onto the **Passeig Marítim**, you come next to the turreted **Sa Llotja** (open Mon–Fri 11am–2pm, 5–9pm when exhibitions are on; free), which was built by Guillem Sagrera in the 15th century as the merchants' stock exchange. Today, this elegant Gothic building is used for art exhibitions, a role for which its beautifully airy interior is well suited.

Continue east along the busy main road to arrive at the prominent statue of the 13th-century Mallorcan philosopher and scientist, **Ramón Llull**. The pedestal dedication is in Catalan, Arabic and Latin, recalling his contributions in all three languages. He stands isolated on a traffic island where the **Passeig de Sagrera** joins the **Avinguda Antoni Maura**, named after a Mallorcan politician of the early 1900s. Here you will find the **S'Hort del Rei** (King's Garden), a beautiful Arabic-style park just beneath the city walls, with pools, fountains and shady greenery, among which stand several arresting modern sculptures, and a bronze *hondero* (the name of the early sling throwers).

At the park's upper end, near Miró's famous sculpture, *Personatge* – always known as The Egg – is a cool modern café that is part of the Palau March *(see page 28)*, which you will pass as you climb the steps leading to the cathedral and the Palau de l'Almudaina *(see page 28)*.

Turn right and then left into the **Plaça de l'Almoina**. Before visiting the cathedral you will see on the left a Mannerist façade dating from the from the 17th century, with interesting details.

Palma's Crowning Glory

The cloister and **Cathedral** (**La Seu**; open Mon–Fri 10am– 6.15pm, Sat 10am–2.15pm; entrance fee) are entered through the **museum** in the Gothic Casa de l'Almoina, which was, in times gone by, a charity house. After the successful invasion of the island in 1229, King Jaume I laid the foundation stone of the new cathedral on the site of the main mosque. Construction took hundreds of years – although the majority of the Gothic structure was finished in the 16th century, the main façade was not completed until the 19th century.

Because the construction of the cathedral took so long, there are examples of several different archi-

Right: several architectural styles are represented in Palma's spectacular cathedral

tectural styles, including 20th-century *Moderniste* touches added by Antoni Gaudí between 1902 and 1914, most notably the extraordinary *baldachino* over the high altar, with a wrought-iron crown of thorns. Many of the 87 windows have been cemented over, but the stained glass on those that survive is wonderful, and the sheer height of the structure gives the interior a spacious feel. There are seven rose windows, the biggest and most beautiful of which has a diameter of 12m (40ft). The **museum**, which keeps the same opening times as the cathedral, and through which you enter the building, features an array of religious artefacts, including Jaume I's innovative portable altar, as well as a splendid silver monstrance and some 14th- and 15th-century works of art. Fragments of the original Roman city can be seen through glass sections of the floor.

The cathedral is impressive from any angle and at any time of day, but bathed in gold by the light of the setting sun, illuminated at night, when seen from a vantage point by the port, or reflected in the lake of the Parc de la Mar below, it is stunning.

Next door to the cathedral is the **Palau de l'Almudaina** (open Mon–Fri 10am–6.30pm, Sat 10am–2pm; entrance fee), the Gothic palace of the Mallorcan kings, built on the site of a Moorish fortress, which was in turn constructed on a Roman site. The palace retains architectural elements from the times of the Arab governors, when Palma was known as Medina Mayurka. Jaume I refashioned the Muslim fortress into a lavish palace. Today it forms part of the National Royal Patrimony and since 1985 has been the official residence of the king of Spain when he is in Mallorca (although he has a private residence to the west of the city). The 14th-century **Capella de Santa Ana** and 13th-century **Sala del Tinell** (Throne Room) are the principal highlights. Some of the walls are decorated with impressive Flemish tapestries, and there is also a very pretty courtyad (Patio del Rei).

The building on the left of the steps (as you leave the Plaça Almoina) is the **Palau March Museu** (open Apr–Oct: Mon–Fri 10–6.30pm; Nov–Mar: till 6pm; Sat 10am–2pm all year; entrance fee. Within this majestic building and its courtyard is housed a superb collection of contemporary sculpture,

including works by Henry Moore, Barbara Hepworth, Rodin and Chillida, and murals by Catalan artist Josep Maria Sert, as well as excellent temporary exhibitions. The palace is also a venue for classical concerts in July and August.

Go back down the steps between the cathedral and the Almudaina. Turn right at the city wall; on the right, before the next set of steps, you pass a pond and a large Gothic arch, the **Arc de la Drassana Reial**, dating from Moorish times, when it was the entrance to the royal shipyards. Following the steps a little way further brings you back to the Parc del Mar, from where there is access to the **Museu Ses Voltes** (open Tues–Sat 10am–5.30pm; free), set into the city walls and devoted to works by contemporary Mallorcan artists.

2. PALMA'S OUTLYING ATTRACTIONS *(see pullout map)*

The remaining attractions, accessible by public transport, lie to the west of the historic centre. They can easily occupy a whole day.

You can get bus No 3 from Plaça Rei Joan Carles to the Plaça Gomilla, from where it is 1-km (1/2-mile) walk to the **Castell de Bellver** (open Apr–Sept: Mon–Sat 8am–8.30pm, Sun 10am–7pm; Oct–Mar: 8am–7.15pm, Sun 10am–5pm; entrance fee), which overlooks the city from a wooded hillside in the city suburb of El Terreno. The 14th-century castle is remarkably well preserved and is considered, along with the cathedral and Sa Llotja, to be among the jewels of Mallorcan architecture. Designed by Pere Salvà, who also worked on the Almudaina Palace, its circular foundation is unique, with three round towers in addition to the central structure. The **Museu d'Història de la Ciutat** within (closed Sunday) documents episodes in Palma's history. Built in a relatively short time, the building exhibits a great unity of Gothic style, but some recent avant-garde additions have raised storms of protest.

From the castle it is an easy walk down through the forest (the largest park in Palma) by way of the steps in front of the main entranceway to have a light and leisurely *tapas* lunch at **Can Salvador** in Plaça S'Aigua Dolça.

Left: Palma's harbour
Above: Castell de Bellver

To the north of the castle, in Palma's western suburbs, is the **Poble Espanyol** (open Apr–Oct: daily 9am–7pm; Nov–Mar: 9am–6pm; entrance fee), where more than 100 replicas of Spain's most famous buildings have been brought together in one walled village. Copies of such well-known buildings as part of the Alhambra of Granada and the Toledo Synagogue rub elbows with the Puerta de Toledo and Seville's Giralda Tower, interspersed with craft workshops, restaurants and pavement cafés. Although well done, it is rather kitsch and a bit of a theme park, but children love it, and it can be fun. (If you are starting your trip from the centre of town, get bus No 5 from Plaça d'Espanya.)

Further out, at Cala Milor, is the **Fundació Pilar i Joan Miró** (open May–Sept: Tues–Sat 10am–7pm; Oct–Apr: 10am– 6pm, Sun 10am–3pm all year; entrance fee), in a streamlined white building, designed by Rafael Moneo, close to the house where the artist lived from 1956 until his death in 1983. His wife, Pilar, was Mallorcan, and as an opponent of the Franco regime, he found life here less restricted than in his native Barcelona. The gallery, surrounded by ponds, is a pleasure in itself, and displays a good selection of the artist's work. Miró's studio, Taller Sert, and his house, San Boter, are currently closed for renovation.

The final place to visit is Palma's newest museum, which is closer than the others to the city centre. If you are getting a bus back along the Passeig Marítim, get off at the Real Club Náutic (the yacht club); if you are starting from the old town, the museum is only a short walk from Sa Llonja. The prestigious **Es Baluard Museu d'Art Modern i Contemporani** (open Jun–Sept: daily 10am–midnight; Oct–May: Tues–Sun 10am–8pm; entrance fee) opened in 2004. It is housed in a stunning white building in Plaça Porta de Santa Catalina,which has wonderful views of the port and the city. Its modern and contemporary displays include a permanent collection of Picasso ceramics as well as works by Tapies, Miró, Dalí, Man Ray, Matisse and Henry Moore and Mallorca's own Miquel Barceló. Since the museum opened, the Santa Catalina area has been rejuvenated, so you can expect to find new bars, cafés, shops and restaurants springing up.

3. ANDRATX AND BANYALBUFAR *(see map, p33)*

The far west of Mallorca, from the gleaming yachts of Port d'Andratx marina to quiet Sant Elm and on to the beautiful northwest coast.

From Palma, head west on the main highway, the PM-1. Bypassing the resorts of Palma Nova, Magaluf and Santa Ponça, the road runs through wooded hills before arriving at the turning for Camp de Mar just past Peguera.

   Camp de Mar lies next to a sheltered bay between Cap des Llamp to the right and Cap Andritxol to the left. The bay's most notable feature is the small islet in the middle, accessible by a wooden bridge. The PM-102 route winds through pine forests which from time to time open up to reveal views of the coast.

Andratx and its Port

Despite many changes, **Port d'Andratx** still retains some of its fishing village charm, courtesy of a beautiful setting and a few remaining buildings from the early years of the 20th century – notable examples are the parish church, **Nostra Senyora del Carme** and the elegant hotel, **Villa Italia**. The extensive marina is full of gleaming yachts, as well as a few trawlers – this is still a working port. The area represents the most expensive real estate in Mallorca, and there are many wealthy German and English home-owners. From the nearby Cap de Sa Mola on a clear day, you may just be able to make out the island of Ibiza. For lunch, try the **Miramar** restaurant, which has been open forever – always a good sign.

   Leave the port by car along the **Andratx** road. In the distance you see the two peaks of the Esclop mountain. The town has been almost forgotten by the tourist industry, because of the attention concentrated on its port. But the parent town collects the taxes and, no doubt, smiles all the way to the bank about the success of her port. Andratx, at the heart of a fertile agricultural region, was founded as a refuge for Christian settlers and was the home of both the Bishop of Barcelona and King Jaume I in the 13th century. At the top of the town, above the Plaça del Pou, are the towering walls of the fortress-like church of **Santa Maria**. The Wednesday morning market at Andratx is one of Mallorca's largest.

   The town's latest attraction, which should bring visitors, is the impressive new **Centro Cultural Andratx**, which stages contemporary art exhibitions in a parkland setting. There are also artists' workshops and a restaurant and bookshop on site (tel: 971 137 770 for details).

   From here, follow the signs for S'Arracó and Sant Elm. On the western edge of Andratx, the *possessió* (country estate) of **Sa Font** still displays

Left: Miró's studio is just as it was when he died
Above: late afternoon winter sunshine at Port d'Andratx

much of the splendour it enjoyed in its heyday as an olive oil producer. The tiny village of **S'Arracó** grew up around the chapel of Sant Crist. A turn-of-the-20th-century guide book tells of the 'cart journey [from here] to Palma lasting nine hours'. The village has the best collection of *indianos* (houses built by Mallorcans returning from the colonies) to be found anywhere on the island. Consequently, the village is an obligatory stop for anyone who is interested in architecture.

Continue on to the quiet village of **Sant Elm**, with a view of the uninhabited island of **Sa Dragonera**. There are boat tours to the island, a national park, several times a day in summer (May–Sept) from the minuscule port. Dragonera offers a wonderful sense of isolation and is popular with walkers and birdwatchers, who come to see the rare Eleanora's Falcon and impressive numbers of seabirds. Sant Elm itself has a reasonable little beach, and there is a good walk north (allow 4 to 5 hours for the round trip) to the ruins of **Sa Trapa monastery**, with wonderful scenery and views over to Sa Dragonera. The other local sight is the **Castell de Sant Elm**, built on the orders of King Jaume II as a hospital for sailors in the latter part of the 13th century.

Along the Northwest Coast

Returning to Andratx, follow the signs for Estellencs. The road climbs in front of the castle of **Son Mas**, originally a Moorish fortress. Continue past the cemetery and into the pine forest where, after passing the highest point, there is often a noticeable change in the climate. Soon, at Km 103, you will be getting out your camera and, at Km 99 you'll see the first building since leaving Andratx – the bar/restaurant **Es Grau** and the **Mirador de Ricard Roca**, with stunning views across the blue Mediterranean. Tour buses habitually stop here to refresh their passengers, so if it's busy we suggest you drive another two or three kilometres and stop for lunch at the **Coll des Pi** restaurant. Here you can look out over the terraced hillsides of Estellencs (pronounced *Es-ta-yencs*).

To reach **Cala Estellencs**, immediately upon entering the village turn sharply downhill to the left onto Carrer Eusebi Pascual, and follow it to the sea. The rocky inlet is ringed by tiny boathouses in which the fishermen keep their nets and gear. Up the hill in the village, the most interesting building is the ancient church of **Sant Joan Bautista**, erected in 1422, but the general look and layout of the little town, which dates back to Arab times, makes it worth a walk around.

Above: the beach at Sant Elm, with the uninhabited island of Sa Dragonera beyond

From the public wash house onwards, the road passes through an array of cultivated terraces on its way to one of the island's best known lookout points, the tower of the **Mirador de Ses Animes**.

Banyalbufar is considered the island's best example of felicitous land use. The terracing of the steep hillsides has been elevated to an art form around the village. On the surrounding embankment the villagers once cultivated the now-legendary *malvasia* wine. Although the wine is no more, its name lives on in local parlance as a synonym for 'marvellous'. The **Hotel Mar-i-Vent** became a summer retreat for many Palma residents during the 1940s, and remains one of the nicest hotels on the island *(see page 92)*. Its restaurant, which serves Mallorcan cuisine, is excellent.

The road from Banyalbufar is well-surfaced and provides a deserved rest for weary drivers. Pass the turning for Port des Canonge, and at the next junction keep right, in the direction of Esporles, and 1.5km (1 mile) further on is the country estate and museum of **Sa Granja** *(see page 60)*.

You will then pass through Esporles along the side of the **Torrent de Sant Pere**. The textile mills that once supported the town have disappeared, and the village is once again living on the bounty of its citrus groves. After leaving the main street of Esporles, turn left at the petrol station and then follow the signs back to Palma.

4. INCA, LLUC AND SA CALOBRA *(see map, p40–41)*

A visit to the leather centre of Inca, then into the beautiful Tramuntana mountains and the pilgrimage centre of Lluc. Afterwards, take the dramatically winding road to reach the north coast at Sa Calobra.

The large town of **Inca** is well known as the centre of the leather industry, and is full of large wholesale outlets. Real bargains are few and far between these days, however, and we can only advise you to shop around. Most of the outlets are located around the main through road, the Avinguda Rei Jaume I, which skirts the town to the south (look out for the Camper signs, for trendy shoes). From the third roundabout along (when approaching from Palma), follow the palm-lined road, signposted to Lluc and Selva, to the **Plaça de Mallorca**; keep left at the end of the square and then bear right at the fork to pass along the right side of the parish church of **Santa Maria la Major**, with a free-standing bell tower. Follow the one-way streets to the **Plaça d'Espanya**, site of the city hall and the elegant **Café Mercantil**. Continue until you are forced to turn left in front of the **Celler Can Ripoll** *(see page 77)*. This restaurant is well known for its delicious Mallorcan dishes, and has a good wine list. Turning left onto Carrer Murta, the street leads back to the **Plaça d'Orient**, from where you follow the signs towards Lluc and Selva.

Into the Mountains

The road to Lluc, the PM-213, provides a postcard view of the parish church of **Selva** against the mountains. The church, the steps to which begin in the **Plaça Major**, contains one or two examples of Gothic religious art.

Following the route north, you will pass under an arched bridge leading to the Selva cemetery. A couple of kilometres further, **Caimari** lays nestled

Above: town band at Lluc monastery

in the foothills. In late summer villagers can be seen in the fields collecting almonds, or sitting by the roadside chatting with neighbours.

The road begins its uphill climb even before leaving the village. It crawls along the right-hand side of the gorge called the **Comellar de sa Cometa Negra**, and you'll see here the island's most dramatic example of hillside terracing, dating back many centuries. After crossing the first pass, you arrive at the **Salt de la Bella Dona**, where it is said a beautiful woman was thrown into the gorge by her husband – but when he arrived back at Lluc, she was waiting to greet him.

Openings in the pine forest provide spectacular views of the **Torrent des Guix**, which skirts the right-hand side of the road. After the petrol station, which serves excellent coffee and pastries in a little café, you have a choice of turning right to visit the **Monestir de Lluc** or going left towards the mountain road to **Sa Calobra**.

Lluc is the religious centre of Mallorca. It is the home of the island's *patrona*, Nostra Senyora de Lluc and, as such, is the annual destination of tens of thousands of pilgrims. But the monastery is interesting to visitors of every creed, both for its historic interest and for the architectural interventions of such famous artists as Antoni Gaudí *(for full details on the monastery see page 44).*

After passing the **Escorca** restaurant on the mountain road towards Sóller (and Sa Calobra), you arrive at a small lookout point. More or less at eye level across the valley you can see the abandoned Guardia Civil barracks and the houses of **Cosconar**, which are built into the cliff face in front of Puig Roig. Beneath you to the right is the Torrent de Lluc and to the left, the Torrent des Gorg Blau. The two join at the Entreforc and together run towards the sea as the spectacular Torrent de Pareis.

Dramatic Descent

Passing under the arches of the aqueduct, turn immediately to the right and follow the signs to Sa Calobra (13km/8 miles). The PMV-2141 is, without doubt, one of the most spectacular roads on the island. Be prepared for it to be very busy in summer, with tour buses as well as private cars. In the distance to the right at the switchback curve, you have a spectacular view of **Puig Roig**, and to the left a breathtaking panorama of the road ahead. At this point the highway begins its descent rather seriously. From time to time you can see the serpentine road basking in the sun like an enormous snake – at one point it twists through 270° to loop underneath itself. Eventually, you will pass the small house of Es Bosc on a flat to the left of the road and, later, the house of Can Pou

Above: the village of Selva in the foothills of the Serra de Tramuntana

where the road divides. At the junction you are greeted by a mass of direction and welcome signs. Turn left and follow the signs to tranquil **Cala Tuent** until you reach a small chapel at the road's highest point. This is the Romanesque **Ermita de Sant Llorenç**, which dates from the 13th century. Considering that this road wasn't indicated on maps made in the late 1950s, the place must have enjoyed almost total isolation for hundreds of years. The view is staggering.

Returning to the junction, turn downhill towards **Sa Calobra**. At the bottom of the road, either park and walk or drive to the left as far as the cul-de-sac and roadside bar. A short walk along the coastal path takes you through two tunnels to emerge at the **Torrent de Pareis**. Close to the end of the short flight of steps which descends from the tunnel to the beach is a small stone stage on which a concert is held in the early summer each year; the adventurous can hike inland a short way between the walls of the gorge. The less adventurous can go for a swim between the cliffs – or just join the many other visitors taking pictures of the view. From the top of Sa Calobra road, the journey back to Palma will take a little over an hour.

5. POLLENÇA AND FORMENTOR *(see maps, p37 and 40–41)*

This route explores the northernmost corner of Mallorca, with a visit to the pleasant town of Pollença and its lively port, before heading on to the spectacular cliffs and quiet coves of the Formentor Peninsula.

From Palma, take the motorway to Inca, continue a further 6km (4 miles) towards Alcúdia, pass **Campanet** and turn left at the *Coves de Campanet* sign, 2½km (1½ miles) further along. You soon arrive at the 13th-century

Oratori de Sant Miquel, which has been declared a national monument, and is a favourite place for weddings and the site of great festivities at Easter. The **Coves de Campanet** (open Apr–Sept: daily 10am–7pm; Oct–Mar: 10am–6pm; entrance fee) are only a short distance from the small chapel. The interiors of the caves are well presented, although there is less to see than at the Artà or Drach caves on the east coast *(see pages 66 and 67)* and they are less commercialised.

Turn right after leaving the parking area onto a secondary road which runs the length of the **Vall de Sant Miquel**. Between the comparatively green foothills to the left of the road appears the domed shape of **Tomir**, Mallorca's third highest mountain at 1,102m (3,615ft).

Left: Pollença old town

Pollença

At the stop sign, turn left onto the PM-220. In the distance are the jagged peaks of the **Serra del Cavall Bernat**. Passing through the shadow of the hilltop hermitage of Nostra Senyora del Puig *(see page 44)*, follow the highway in its right-hand curve until you see a roundabout on the right. From the monument, dedicated to Pollensian poet Miquel Costa i Llobera, follow the *Centro* signs into **Pollença**, along the Via Pollentia towards the bell tower of the parish church. It is best to park the car nearby and walk.

The central square, **Plaça Major**, is always busy but on Sunday it is a hive of activity, with the weekly market taking up any space not used by the outdoor cafés. The 14th-century parish church on the square, **La Mare de Déu des Àngels**, was built by the Knights Templar. There's a modern art gallery here, too, **Galería Bennassar** (open Mon–Sat 10am–1pm, 5–8.30pm, Sun 10am–1pm; entrance fee). The steps of the **Via Crucis** lead up between cypress trees from beside the church to **El Calvari**, a tiny chapel on the hill. The 365-step climb is tiring, but worthwhile (although it is also possible to drive up). Although the oratory at the top only dates from the 19th century, it houses a statue of the Virgin at the feet of Christ some 500 years older. On Good

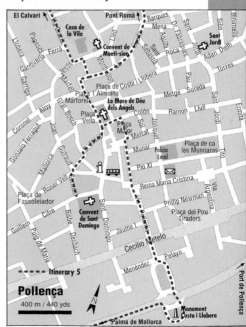

Pollença

400 m / 440 yds

---- Itinerary 5

Above: the calm waters of the Badia de Pollença

Friday a figure of Jesus is carried down the steps to the parish church in a sombre ceremony.

A short distance south of the square is the deconsecrated **Convent de Sant Domingo** (church, cloister and museum open Tues–Sat 10.30am–1pm, 5.30pm–midnight (earlier in winter), Sun 10.30am–1pm; entrance fee), which was built by the Dominicans in the 17th century. The outstanding cloister is the venue for a prestigious music festival in summer. The **Museu Municipal** within the convent has a rather eclectic art collection, including some good Gothic pieces. Another interesting building is the **Convent de Montesión**, built by the Jesuits in 1738 in the baroque style of the day. Next to it is the Ajuntament (Town Hall), once a Jesuit college; and nearby is the little Plazuela de la Almoina with a central fountain topped with a cockerel, the symbol of the town.

If you skirt the centre of town by car and reach the Carrer Huerto, you can visit the **Pont Romà** as you leave for the port. Although the origins of the bridge are obscure, it is thought to be part of the canal system built by the Romans in the 2nd century AD.

Down to the Port

Continue along the road and turn right towards **Port de Pollença** at the next junction. Getting to the heart of the port is simply a matter of not changing direction until you get to the water's edge. The seafront is lined

with a long row of restaurants and hotels – some of which, like Sis Pins and the Miramar, have maintained their original charm. There is usually plenty going on in Port de Pollença – ask at the tourist office or at a hotel reception. Some of the restaurants serve *caldereta de llagosta* (a rich, and expensive, lobster stew), which originates in Menorca.

Don't be fooled by the morning stillness of the bay. The habitual *gregal* – northeast wind – has blessed the place as a windsurfers' paradise. Athletes such as Eduardo Bellini, many times Spanish and European champion, come from here; for visitors, lessons and equipment are advertised.

A possible walking excursion from Port de Pollença is the beach at **Cala Bóquer**, an hour and a half's stroll through the attractive Vall de Bóquer.

The Formentor Peninsula

Port de Pollenca's Carretera de Formentor, one street behind the front-line Carrer Anglada Camarasa, runs parallel to the curve of the waterfront in the direction of the **Formentor Peninsula**. The highway, the PM-221, makes a hard left turn at the airforce base and begins to climb quite quickly until it arrives at the **Mirador des Colomer**. The view down to the small island of **El Colomer** is one of the best known on Mallorca. The road runs in and out of rocks and pine forest, switching from one side of the peninsula to the other, providing spectacular views of the Badia de Pollença and the Mediterranean. At the turning for the Hotel Formentor *(see below)*, keep left and continue east through the woods towards the **Cap de Formentor** (11km/7 miles), the northeastern tip of the island.

On one flat stretch passing between low rock walls, you can see the old houses of **Cases Velles de Formentor**, which was where one of Pollença's most famous citizens, the poet Costa i Llobera, spent much of his life. Pass-

ing above **Cala Figuera**, to the left you can see in the distance a lone pine tree. For the Mallorcans it calls to mind one of the poet's most famous poems, *Es pi de Formentor*.

Continue through the tunnels to the lighthouse at Cap de Formentor. The views out to sea from here are tremendous. The first headland visible to the right (southeast) is **Cap des Pinar**, which divides the Badia de Pollença from the Badia d'Alcúdia. Beyond that is the peak of **Cap Ferrutx**, and further towards the horizon is the headland of **Cap des Freu**. This is a great spot for birdwatching during the spring and autumn migrations, and on a clear day you can see Menorca, 25 nautical miles to the east. There is a café at the lighthouse. Return along the peninsula to the **Hotel Formentor** *(see page 91)*, Mallorca's original luxury hotel which has hosted international celebrities such as Charlie Chaplin and Grace Kelly. The beach is marvellous, with fine sands and lovely views across the bay. Return to Palma via Pollença and Inca, approximately 1 hour 15minutes' drive.

Above Left: Pont Romà dates from the 2nd century AD
Left: wonderful views at El Colomer. **Above:** Formentor lighthouse

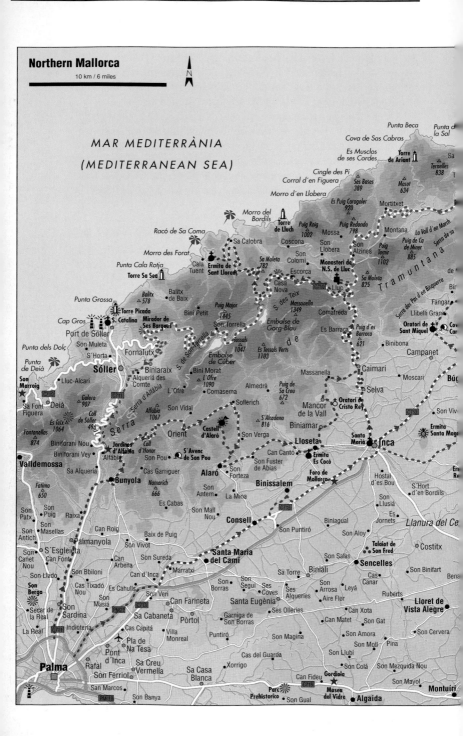

Northern Mallorca

10 km / 6 miles

N

MAR MEDITERRÀNIA
(MEDITERRANEAN SEA)

Punta Beca
Cova de Sas Cabras
Punta de la Sal
Es Musclos de ses Cordes
Torre de Ariant
Sa
Ternelles 838
Cingle des Pi
Corral d'en Figuera
Ses Bases 389
Masat 634
Morro d'en Llobera
Es Puig Caragoler 920
Mortitxet
Morro del Bordils
Torre de Lluch
Puig Roig 1002
Mossa
Montana
La Vall d'en March
Racó de Sa Coma
Sa Calobra
Coscona
Son Llobera
Puig de Ca de Miner 885
Morro des Forat
Cala Tuent
Sa Moleta 782
Son Colomi
Son Alzines
Puig Tomir 1102
Punta Cala Rotja
Cala Tuent
Ermita de Sant Llorenc
Escorca
Monasteri de N.S. de Lluc
Torre Sa Sea
Casa Nova
Lluc
Sa Moleta 825
Tramuntana
Punta Grossa
Balitx 578
Balitx de Baix
Puig des Teix
Massanella 1349
Serra des Pas d'en Bisquerra
Torre Picada
Bini Petit
Comafreda
Llibelli Gran
Cap Gros
S. Catalina
Mirador de Ses Barques
Puig Major 1445
Son Torrella
Embalse de Gorg-Blau
Es Barraca
Puig d'es Barraca 621
Oratori de Sant Miquel
Port de Sóller
Son Muleta
Tossals 1047
Binibona
Campanet
Punta dels Dolç
S'Horta
Fornalutx
Embalse de Cúber
Es Tossals Verts 1103
Caimari
Moscari
Búg
Punta de Deià
Sóller
Biniaraix
Bini Morat
Massanella
Selva
Son Viv
Son Marroig
Lluc-Alcari
Alquería des Comte
L'Ofre 1090
Almedrà
Ermita Santa Mag
Sa Font Figuera
Deià
Galera 907
L'Ofre
Comasema
Puig de Sa Creu 672
Oratori de Cristo Rey
Es Teix 1064
Coll de Sóller 496
Son Vidal
Sollerich
S'Alcadena 816
Mancor de la Vall
Santa María
Inca
Fontanellas 874
Biniforani Nou
Alfàbia 1067
Castell d'Alaró
Son Verga
Biniamar
Biniforani Vey
Jardines d'Alfàbia
Coll d'Honor
Son Pou
S'Avenc de Son Pou
Lloseta
Ermita Es Cocó
Em
R
Valldemossa
Alfàbia
Cas Garriguer
Alaró
Son Forteza
Foro de Mallorca
Hostal d'es Bou
S'Hort d'en Bordils
Sa Alqueria
Cas Garriguer
Son Antem
Son Fuster de Abias
Binissalem
Son Llusià
Es Jornets
Fátima 650
Bunyola
Namarich 666
La Miña
Biniagual
Llanura del Ce
Son Patx
Son Puig
Es Cabas
Son Mall Nou
Consell
Son Puntiró
Son Aloy
Costitx
Son Antich
Son Masellas
Can Roig
Baix de Puig
Son Vivot
Son Safas
Talaiot de Son Fred
Son Binifart
Bena
Palmanyola
Raixa
Can Arbena
Can d'Inca
Marratxi
Santa Maria del Camí
Sa Torre
Biniali
Sencelles
Cas Canar
S'Esgleieta
Can Font
Son Bbiloni
Son Sureda
Son Segui
Ses Coves
Son Arrosa
Leyá
Ruberts
Lloret de Vista Alegre
Son Canet Nou
Son Lladó
Cas Tixadó Nou
Es Cahulls
Can Veri
Ses Alqueries
Aire Flor
Can Xota
Son Gat
Son Berga
Son Masià
Can Farineta
Santa Eugènia
Ses Ollèries
Can Matet
Son Amora
Son Cervera
Secar de la Real
Son Sardina
Indioteria
Sa Cabaneta
Pòrtol
Garniga de Son Borras
Son Magina
Son Moll
Pina
La Real
Rafal
Villa Monreal
Puntiró
Cas del Guarda
Son Llubi
Son Colá
Son Mezquida Nou
Pla de Na Tesa
Son Ferriol
Sa Creu Vermella
Sa Casa Blanca
Xorrigo
Can Fideu
Gordiola
Son Mayol
Montuïri
Palma
San Marcos
Son Banya
Parc Prehistoric
Son Gual
Museu del Vidre
Algaida

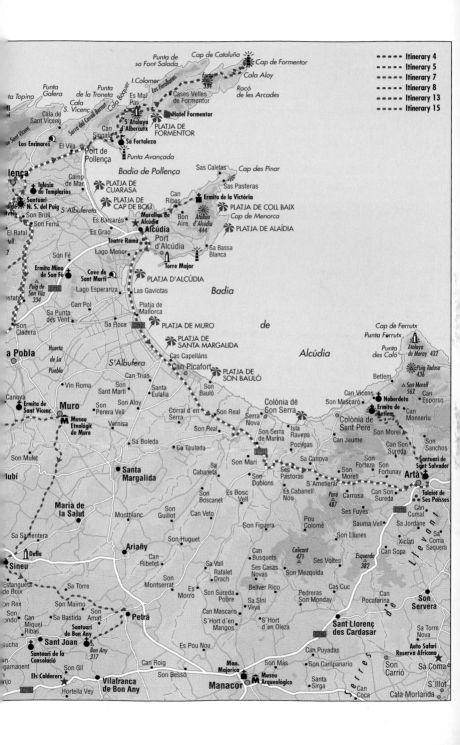

Itinerary 4
Itinerary 5
Itinerary 7
Itinerary 8
Itinerary 13
Itinerary 15

6. HERMITAGES OF THE CENTRAL PLAIN *(see map, p43)*

A tour of the southern region of the central *pla*, with hilltop monasteries, an 18th-century manor and the island's oldest glassworks.

Since the day King Jaume I reconquered Mallorca in the name of Christianity, the most religious among the population have sought out special places at which to worship or meditate. Some have found their solitude in caves, others on the island's highest peaks. Apart from a notable exception in Cala Portals Vells, the caves have all been lost. But the hilltop hermitages have not only survived, they have prospered in recent years as sanctuaries and monasteries and are fascinating places to visit.

There is a concentration of them on the hills that rise out of the central plain south of the main Palma to Manacor road. For those further east, around Santanyi and Felanitx, *see pages 68-69.*

Montesión to Randa

Just to the west of the town of **Porreres**, off the Llucamajor road, the Via Crusis leads up to the **Santuari de Montesió**. The Gothic style sanctuary houses a 15th-century marble statue of the Virgin, along with many reminders of its days as a grammar school between the 16th and 19th centuries.

From Porreres, follow the PM-503 north towards **Montuíri**. After passing the church of **Santa Creu** and the municipal cemetery, continue along a narrow road part bounded by stone walls. At the Palma–Manacor road, turn right. At Km37, just past the turning for Sant Joan, is another left turn which leads to the 18th-century country estate of **Els Calderers de Sant Joan** (open Apr–Oct: daily 10am–6pm; Nov–Mar 10am–5pm; entrance fee). You can tour the estate, the house, chapel and granary and sample homemade products. The opulent decoration of the house illustrates the considerable wealth enjoyed by the Mallorcan landed gentry. This was an important wine-growing area until the outbreak of *phylloxera* in 1870 forced a switch to cereal production.

Return to the main road and turn right towards Palma. Passing Montuíri and its old stone windmills on the right, you will see a sign on the left indicating **Randa** (6km/4 miles). A road winds its way up the Puig de Randa, leading to Randa's three oratories. The first is the **Oratori de Nostra Senyora de Gràcia**, built into an enormous cave in the cliff face, with a tremendous view of the plain below. The interior is baroque and holds an interesting collection of altarpieces and paintings. Less interesting, but in better condition, is the oratory of **Sant Honorat**, slightly higher up the road.

Nostra Senyora de Cura crowns the mountain. The fortress-like structure is made up of a series of monastic cells (in which accommodation is

Above: Mallorca's interior villages have hardly changed over the years
Above Right: glassware at Gordiola

available, tel: 971 120 260), a church, a small garden and the **Museum and Gramática of Ramón Llull** (open daily 10am–1pm, 4–6pm; free) dedicated to Mallorca's 13th-century philosopher and teacher (1235–1316). There is an open picnic area and restaurant here as well.

After leaving Rand, a head north to Algaida, well known for its restaurants – we recommend the **Hostal d'Algaida** (next to the petrol station on the main road), **Can Dimoni** (House of the Devil) for a rustic but authentic Mallorcan meal (also on the main road) and **Es Cuatre Vents** (next to Can Dimoni).

Shortly after leaving Algaida on the Palma road, you can't miss the large mock castle, dating from the 1960s. This is the **Gordiola Museu del Vidre** (open Apr–Oct: Mon–Sat 9am–8pm; Nov–Mar 9am–1.30pm, 3–7pm; Sun 9am–1pm; free), a glassworks and museum where you can see the glass being melted and blown by skilled craftsmen – their works are for sale in the adjacent showroom. The **museum**, displaying Gordiola pieces dating from the early 18th century, as well a collection of antique glass items from all over Europe.

Southern Mallorca

- - - Itinerary 6
- - - Itinerary 12

10 km / 6 miles

7. MOUNTAIN PASSAGE *(see map, p40–41)*

A tour of the spectacular Serra de Tramuntana, with visits to the sacred monastery at Lluc and the attractive village of Fornalutx.

From the Inca–Alcúdia road, take the turn-off for Pollença/Port de Pollença. The route runs north through pine-covered hills, with views over the picturesque valley to the jagged peaks of the **Serra de Sant Vicenç** in the background. As you approach Pollença, on top of a steep hillside to the right is the 14th-century hermitage of **Nostra Senyora del Puig**. It is possible to stay here (tel: 971 184 132), but the road only extends halfway up the mountain so getting to the monastery involves a stiff climb. The view, of course, is absolutely stunning. **Pollença** itself is worth a long visit, but

with almost the entire *cordillera* ahead of you it is better to leave it for another day *(see page 37)*. Skirt around the town along the bypass, following signs for Lluc and Sóller.

The rocky **Serra de Tramuntana** mountains run right along the north coast of Mallorca, and the well-surfaced C-710 threads its way through almost their full extent, from Pollença to Andratx. Heading west from Pollença you will soon see **Puig Tomir**, at 1,102m (3,615ft) the third-highest peak on the island. After passing the recreational area at Km16, a petrol station sign alerts you to the upcoming entrance to the Monestir de Lluc, less than a kilometre ahead.

Top: rocky ridges in the Serra de Tramuntana
Above: the baroque facade of Lluc monastery

itineraries

Pilgrimage Centre

Greeted by a sign saying *Benvinguts* (Welcome), walk through an enormous stone entrance leading into the gardens of the **Plaça dels Peregrins** (Pilgrims' Square). One of the many buildings lining the square is the town hall of the 'villa' of Escorca, the only municipality in Mallorca that doesn't have an urban nucleus.

The **Monestir de Lluc** (open Apr–Sept: daily 10am–6.30pm; Oct–Mar: 10am–5.30pm) is the home of the Congregation of the Sacred Heart, a hospice and a museum. Pilgrims have been coming here for almost 800 years to see the statuette of the Virgin de Lluc, La Moreneta (The Little Dark One). According to legend, the figurine was discovered in the woods by a shepherd boy, Lluc, who took it to a local church; the statue kept miraculously returning to the same spot, so a chapel was built to house it. La Moreneta continues to attract thousands of pilgrims, and in August there is an overnight pilgrimage from Palma. At 11am Mass each day you can hear the wonderful sound of the Lluc boys' choir, the Coro Blavets (The Blue Ones), named after the colour of their cassocks.

The baroque façade of the church hides an interior renovated by Moderniste architects Gaudí, Rubió and Reynés, who were also involved in the construction of the *rosario* that winds up the hill behind the monastery. This path leads to the crucifix at the top of the hill (about 10 minutes' walk) from where there are lovely views over the valley and, in the other direction, to Puig Roig. It is possible to stay overnight at the monastery, in basic accommodation, but you need to book ahead (tel: 971 517 025/971 871 525). There is arestaurant as well as a communal kitchen for pilgrims and hikers who want to prepare their own meals.

Returning to the main road you soon arrive at the turn-off for Palma/Inca and the petrol station. Follow the sign towards Sa Calobra and Sóller (22 and 32km/14 and 20 miles respectively). From here you set out on a long scenic drive that roughly follows the left side of the **Torrent de Lluc**. Not far past the popular **Restaurante Escorca**, you arrive at a lookout point where there's a good overview not only of the Torrent de Lluc, but also of **Puig Roig** and the **Entreforc**, where Mallorca's famous **Torrent de Pareis** begins.

The road begins a gentle descent. Ahead is **Puig Major**, the island's highest peak at 1,445m (4,740ft). The road runs along the **Torrent des Gorg Blau** until it eventually crosses a bridge and passes under an aqueduct. Leaving the long twisting road to Sa Calobra for another trip *(see pages 35–36),* you continue on the C-713. After passing through a tunnel you will find a stopping area where you can view the **Embalse des Gorg Blau**, one of the two principal reservoirs in the Mallorcan water supply system. Behind the reservoir is the island's second highest mountain, **Massanella**, as well as **Tossals** and **L'Ofre**.

Soon afterwards comes the second link in the water chain, the **Embalse de Cúbert**, and the military base

Right: statue of the Virgin at Lluc museum

at the foot of Puig Major. A second tunnel marks the highest point along this route, with a view of the **Vall de Sóller**. On the ear-popping descent you will pass the **Mirador de Ses Barques**, from where there is a bird's-eye-view of Port de Sóller, before arriving at the turning to Fornalutx.

Spain's Prettiest Village

Fornalutx, with steep stone streets and centuries-old houses, is considered one of the best-kept villages in Mallorca, and has been described as the prettiest in Spain. The parish church dates from 1639, and many of the houses still retain remnants of Moorish paintings under the eaves. The stunning mountain location, with views down the valley to Sóller, has made Fornalutx very popular with expats – mainly German and British – who own a high proportion of the property hereabouts; prices have risen sharply over the past few years.

Leave the village by way of Carrer de Sant Bartomeu and descend through the lemon groves towards Sóller in the distance. As the road curves left, it leads across a riverbed to a junction where there is a large stone cross and a modern house (Ca Sa Creu) which marks, more or less, the beginning of Sóller.

Because of its geographical isolation from the rest of Mallorca, Sóller is unusual among the island's towns. It is worth wandering around it and taking a trip to the port (*see page 54*). The town is only 30km (18 miles) from Palma, but the giant wall of the Serra d'Alfàbia makes it feel considerably further, even since the opening of the tunnel in 1997 which cuts the drive time from 50 minutes to 30. If you have time, take the old route over the pass. After climbing 25 hairpin bends, you pass an elegant country house, at the back of which is the Font des Teix mineral water bottling plant. At the 30th bend you will reach the **Coll de Sóller**. The way down is easier – there are only 28 hairpin bends. After the final turn is the elegant mansion of **Alfàbia** with its fabulous gardens (*see page 49*). Leaving the mountains of the Serra de Tramuntana in your rear view mirror, drive towards the silhouette of Palma in the distance.

8. MALLORCA'S INTERIOR *(see map, p40–41)*

A tour of the island's little-known interior attractions, including wine tasting in Binissalem, lunch in a traditional *celler*, and a visit to Junípero Serra's birthplace.

Away from the coasts, the quiet countryside and ancient towns of the Mallorcan interior have remained largely unaffected by tourism, and offer considerable rewards to those who make the effort to go and find them.

Carrer Aragó takes you out of Palma and, via a dogleg directed by signs to Inca, leads you onto the PM-27 motorway. At a flyover, 8km (5 miles) further on, follow the signs to **Santa Maria del Camí**. At No 77 on the main through road is the **Artesania Textil Bujosa**, a well-known manufacturer of traditional Mallorcan cloth. The cloth is known as *roba de llengües* because of its multi-coloured, tongue-shaped designs. Not far away, with its enormous bell tower, is the 17th-century **Convent dels Mínimas** and the house and museum of **Can Conrado**. The parish church of Santa Maria, situated in the **Plaça Caidos**, has a baroque bell tower sheathed in blue ceramic tiles, reminiscent of the one in Valldemossa.

The route to Consell and Binissalem provides a good opportunity to view the table-top mountain of Alaró *(see page 58)*. **Binissalem** is the centre of the island's wine industry (visit **Bodega de José L Ferrer**), introduced by the Romans. Turn left off the unattractive main road into the compact centre, where there are such historic sights as **Can Gelabert** and **Can Garriga**, the 18th-century parish church and the old cemetery, once the site of a mosque.

Further along the main road, opposite the turning to Lloseta, you come to the **Foro de Mallorca** complex, with its mini-golf course, go-kart arena, water-park and wax museum.

Across *Es Pla*

Follow the road around Inca to the south *(see page 34)*, turning right for Muro at the fourth roundabout. The road winds its way across the farmland of the central plain *(pla)*, passing the hilltop hermitage of Santa Magdalena on the left. Once in **Muro**, make your way to the central Plaça Constitució, where the unusual-looking church of **Sant Joan Bautista** has a bell tower connected to the main building by a small, graceful arch. The **Museu Etnológic*** (open Apr–Sept: Tues–Sat 10am–2pm, 5–8pm, Sun 10am–1pm; Oct–Mar: 10am–1pm, entrance fee) is nearby in the old mansion of Can Alomar, at Carrer Major 15. This is one of the best museums on the island, with a large collection of memorabilia, agricultural implements and ceramics.

Above Left: Fornalutx village crest with its kiln. **Left:** *al fresco* in Fornalutx
Above: the autumn grape harvest

To leave Muro in the direction of Sineu, follow the signs for Santa Margalida. Two hundred metres (220yds) after joining the PM-343 turn right at the crossroads towards Sineu (11km/7 miles). The PMV-3442 passes through bucolic countryside until it arrives in **Sineu**, at the centre of the island.

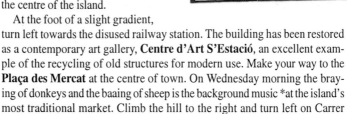

At the foot of a slight gradient, turn left towards the disused railway station. The building has been restored as a contemporary art gallery, **Centre d'Art S'Estació**, an excellent example of the recycling of old structures for modern use. Make your way to the **Plaça des Mercat** at the centre of town. On Wednesday morning the braying of donkeys and the baaing of sheep is the background music *at the island's most traditional market. Climb the hill to the right and turn left on Carrer

Església, which leads into **Plaça Santa Catalina Tomàs** and **Plaça d'Espanya**, with the Gothic parish church of **Santa Maria de Sineu**.

One of the town's most spectacular buildings is **Can Garriga**, which fronts onto **Plaça Sant Marcos**, a short flight of stone steps down from the side of the parish church. Among other small palaces which lend Sineu a rustic charm is **Son Torelló (Toreó)**, now a restaurant on the street of the same name, and various *cellers* (pronounced *say-airs)* serving traditional wine and food in cavernous basement dining rooms, such as the **Celler Sa Font** in the Plaça d'Espanya.

In Costitx, 7km (4 miles) west of Sineu, the Planetarium (open Mon–Fri 10am–2pm, 4–6pm; entrance fee) is entertaining and educational.

The Home of Fray Junípero Serra
The road to Petra runs along the valley towards Puig de sa Creu mountain. As you enter the town you will see the new **Ca N'Oms** (open Mon–Sat 11am–1pm, 6–10pm; free), a modern art gallery with a pleasant sculpture garden and a smart bar. The nearby church of Sant Pere is where Petra's famous son, Fray Junípero Serra, was baptised on 24 November 1713. Serra established several missions in California that have grown into cities, including San Francisco (founded in 1776). Directly across the road from the church is the rectory with a small garden of ruined arches and statue of Valldemossan Catalina Tomàs, Mallorca's only saint.

On Carrer Major, one block past the junction with Carrer California, is the **Convent de Sant Bernardí**, where Serra was educated. Carrer Junípero Serra, which runs beside the convent, leads to the **Casa Museu Fray Juníper Serra** (opening times vary; a notice outside tells you where to get the key;

Top: ceramic plaques in Petra commemorate Junípero Serra's Californian missions
Above: Serra's humble birthplace

donation requested). The museum, run by a dedicated Society of Friends, illustrates the Californian and other New World missions; his house next door is more interesting, a modest place with cell-like rooms and a pretty garden.

To leave town, follow the signs to Palma and then look for a right turn on a minor road to the **Santuari de Bon Any** (Sanctuary of the Good Year) built in 1600 by local people, grateful for a year of plentiful rains and bountiful harvests. This spectacularly located hermitage was the place where Fray Junípero Serra preached his final sermon before setting off for the New World; it was largely rebuilt in the 1920s.

9. SOLLER TO VALLDEMOSSA *(see maps below and p33)*

A day spent exploring the spectacular mountains and coastline north of Palma, from the pleasant town of Sóller to the Carthusian monastery at Valldemossa via the picturesque artists' and writers' hangout of Deià.

Leaving Palma by way of Carrer 31 de Desembre and highway C-711, follow the signs to Sóller. Continue straight, up a gradual incline and just before you reach the Sóller tunnel you will see a sign for the **Jardins d'Alfàbia** (open Sept–May: Mon–Fri 9.30am–5.30pm, Sat 9.30am–1pm; Jul–Aug: until 6.30pm; entrance fee) which surround a grand country mansion. Beyond the baroque façade, the entrance is crowned with a *mudéjar* ceiling dating from the 14th century. The house itself dates from the latter part of the 18th century, while the fabulous surrounding grounds are the sum of a group of smaller gardens which reflect everything from the Arab *huerto* (kitchen garden) to the romantic gardens of the mid-19th century. There is a beautiful covered walkway, lily ponds and an orange grove. Next to the gardens is the esteemed Ses Porxeres restaurant *(see page 76)*.

Back in the car, you could take the old road over the **Coll de Sóller**, or the 3-km (2-mile) tunnel (toll) which opened in 1997 and dramatically cuts journey times between Palma and Sóller. The pass offers great views back to Palma, but the road is vertiginous and slow going, with 28 hairpin bends on the way up and 30 more on the other side.

Citrus Centre

The town of **Sóller** enjoys a wonderful setting at the foot of the steep mountains, surrounded by orange and lemon groves. In common with most towns in Mallorca, however, it has many extremely narrow one-way streets – park the car in one of the signposted car parks and make your way into the centre of town

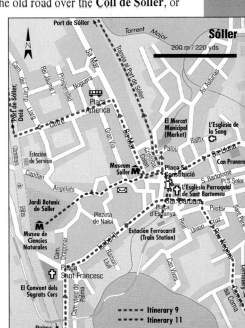

on foot. The attractive main square is the **Plaça Sa Constitució**. The façade of both the church of Sant Bartomeu and the Banco Central Hispano on the opposite corner are two of the town's many examples of *Modernista* architecture. Walk down Carrer Sa Lluna to get an idea of the town's narrow streets, then follow the tram tracks towards the market, passing small, well-tended gardens.

Graves and Marble Temples

To leave town in the direction of Deià and Valldemossa, follow the signs for Port de Sóller. Once on the main road, turn right, and a few hundred metres further you will see the turn-off for Deià to the left. About 4km (2½ miles) further on you will pass over the highest point on the road. Drive between two old houses and find a turning signposted to the Bens D'Avall restaurant *(see page 77)*. Continue past the tiny coastal hamlet of **Llucalcari** before reaching **Deià**, set against the steep rocky slopes of Puig Es Teix. Things can get a bit crowded in the summer, so try to avoid busy times of day during peak season. Walk up the winding carrer Es Puig, just on the right as you enter the village from Sóller, to the hilltop **Església de Sant Joan Bautista**, beside which is the cemetery – the resting place of Mallorca's most famous adopted son. The small flat stone says simply: 'Robert Graves, Poeta, 1895–1985'. The view over the terraced hillside to the sea is wonderful. As might be expected, Graves acted as a magnet for many would-be painters and writers (as well as some more established names, such as Anaïs Nin), and the village has amassed a small colony of artists of varying abilities. Back down the hill is the **Deià Archaeology Museum and Research Center** (open Tues, Fri, Sun 5.30–7pm; entrance fee), set up by Graves and American painter and archaeologist William Waldren in the 1960s. You can reach the local beach, Cala Deià by following this road

Above: the clifftop marble temple in the grounds of Son Morroig (about 35 minutes' walk from the Valldemossa end of the village) or by a short drive down a vertiginous road, from the Sóller end. The beach is small and rocky, but attractive, with a couple of café/restaurant.

To the west of Deià the road begins its climb towards Son Marroig (open Mon–Sat 9am–8pm; entrance fee). Once owned by the Archduke Ludwig Salvator of Habsburg-Lorraine and Bourbon, who had a life-long love affair with the Balearics, the house contains many souvenirs of his days in Mallorca, and is the epitome of an 18th-century seignorial mansion. In the garden is a small marble temple, from which there is a splendid view of Na Foradada, a rocky promontory, pierced by a natural window.

On to Valldemossa

The coastal C-710 continues south, with stunning sea views to the right, and groves of ancient, gnarled olive trees among huge boulders to the left.

Turning left just past the petrol station, it is less than a minute's drive through a long line of sycamore trees to Valldemossa. There are a series of car parks on the left side of the road. This village has been home to four famous people: Mallorca's only saint, Santa Catalina Tomàs, the Archduke Ludwig Salvator and, briefly, Frédéric Chopin and George Sand (see page 51).

The obligatory sights here are the Carthusian Monastery, **La Real Cartuja**, and the **Palau de Rei Sanxo** *(see page 52)*, but if you don't spend an hour walking through the old town you have missed the essence of Valldemossa. The narrow, smooth-stoned streets around **Plaça Sant Catalina Tomàs**, their walls festooned with potted flowers, have inspired numerous artists. Stop for a coffee and a local speciality, *coca de patata (see page 75)*, in Plaça Ramón Llull or Carrer Blanquera, which is lined with cafés.

Leaving town along the Palma road (after passing some interesting little shops selling clothes made of natural fibres), you will see directly ahead of you an elegant building with a square tower. This is **Sa Coma**, another of the Archduke's possessions. The road then winds down the valley to the plain.

10. VALLDEMOSSA *(see map, p52)*

A tour of Valldemossa, Mallorca's highest town and one-time home to Frédéric Chopin, George Sand, Archduke Luis Salvador and Sant Catalina Tomàs.

Coming to Mallorca without visiting Valldemossa would be, to say the least, a great oversight. Of Arab origin, this is the highest large town in Mallorca at 425m (1,395ft), and has played host to a long list of interesting and creative people over the past two centuries. The town was first 'internationalised'

Above: Valldemossa's famous skyline

following the visit of Frédéric Chopin and writer George Sand in the winter of 1838–9. Later it became one of many residences of the Archduke Luis Salvador (Ludwig Salvator) of Austria, who loved Mallorca. Other residents or guests have included the early 20th-century politician Antonio Maura, the Spanish philosopher Miguel de Unamuno and Nicaraguan poet Rubén Darío. Valldemossa was also the birthplace of Catalina Tomàs, Mallorca's only saint. These famous residents have left it rich in both history and anecdote.

SANTA CATALINA THOMAS PREGAU PER NOSALTRES

The Monastery

Approaching from Palma, you will find car parks on the right-hand side of the main road as you enter the urban area. Make your way on foot to the main street, carrer Blanquerna, lined with cafés and gift shops, then turn right to reach Valldemossa's best-known sight, **La Real Cartuja de Valldemossa** (open Mar–Oct: Mon–Sat 9.30am–6pm, Sun 10am–1pm; Nov–Feb: 9.30am–4.30pm; entrance fee includes admission to Museu Municipal and Palau de Rei Sanxo). In 1309 King Jaume II built a palace here, which was used by his asthmatic son, Sanxo. Ninety years later, King Martí of Aragón gave the palace to the Carthusian Order to found a monastery. In the early 18th century, the monks decided the building was inadequate for their needs, and work was begun on the larger structure which stands today. The impressive building, although basically baroque, exhibits a number of neoclassical characteristics. The monks were forced to abandon the monastery in 1835 under the disentailment laws, and the structure was divided and sold at public auction.

The entrance leads you straight into the church, with its frescoes by Fray Manuel Bayeu, brother-in-law of Goya. Around the corner is the Apothecary, which functioned as the town's medical centre until 1896 and is full of the glass bottles and ceramic jars in which the various tonics, lotions and unguents were stored. Past the Prior's Cell (complete with a life-size model of a prior) are the rooms that Chopin and Sand rented during their short stay at the monastery, from 15 December 1838 to 12 February 1839. Their time here was somewhat disastrous, but nevertheless resulted in a series of compositions by the Polish composer and a book, *A Winter in Mallorca*, by Sand, in which she praised the landscape but scorned the people.

Above: memorial plaques to Mallorca's saint adorn Valldemossa's streets

It is sold everywhere in Valldemossa, as well as in the monastery itself. A collection of memorabilia, including letters, paintings and the piano on which Chopin composed the *Raindrop Prelude*, is on display.

Further along is the Museu Municipal. Downstairs are exhibits relating to the Archduke Salvador's work on the island as well as an art gallery featuring paintings of the Serra de Tramuntana. Upstairs is a noteworthy collection of contemporary art, including works by Miró and Picasso, Max Ernst and Antoni Saura.

Leave the monastery and cross the square to the **Palau del Rei Sanxo** (hours as for La Cartuja), constructed in the 16th century on the site of the one Jaume II built for his son, but largely rebuilt in the 18th and 19th centuries, when it was enlarged in the neo-Gothic style and furnished according to the times. You enter through a tranquil, plant-filled courtyard before reaching the theatre, converted from the old chapel, where piano recitals of Chopin's music are held throughout the day.

Shrine to a Saint

It is a short walk to the 1245 parish church of **Sant Bartomeu**. Although the actual construction was begun in the 14th century, the façade wasn't finished until 500 years later. Near the church at Carrer Rectoria 5 is a tiny chapel built where **Santa Catalina** was born in 1531. It was converted into an oratory in 1792. Every year, on 28 July, a young girl from the village is honoured as the *Beatà* (The Beatified One) in a procession.

Back on the main road, the **Centro Cultural Costa Nord** (open daily 9am–6pm; entrance fee), set up by actor Michael Douglas, features an audiovisual presentation on the history of the area and the people who have shaped it. There is a replica of the interior of the Archduke Salvador's boat, the *Nixe*, and a display of books, photographs and drawings of the Serra de Tramuntana mountain landscapes.

Above: view from the Palau del Rei Sanxo

11. PALMA–SOLLER RAILWAY *(see maps, p28 and 33)*

Take the antique train over the mountains to Sóller, with its Moderniste buildings and attractive gardens, before continuing on to the port in the equally old-fashioned *tramvia*.

One of the most enjoyable excursions on Mallorca is to take the antique electric train from Palma to Sóller, which departs from the *fin de siécle* station in Palma's **Plaça d'Espanya** and climbs over the mountains via a series of tunnels to descend into the lovely Sóller Valley.

Trains leave Palma six times a day (seven on Sunday) and take about an hour to reach Sóller. The only difference between the tourist train (at 10.40am and 12.15pm) and the others is that it stops for 10 minutes at the **Mirador del Pujol den Banya** to allow you more time to enjoy the tremendous view of Sóller, its valley, and the mountains beyond, but the price is double that of the usual trip.

The journey ends at the splendid *Moderniste* station on the **Plaça d'Espanya**. From here you can either walk the short distance into the town centre or catch the *tramvia* to Port de Sóller from its starting point in front of the station *(see following page)*.

Follow the tram tracks down the hill a short distance to the pleasant main square,

Top: Sóller and its valley seen from the train
Above: the train is a tourist favourite

the **Plaça Constitució**, dominated by the church of **Sant Bartomeu** (open Mon–Thur 10.30am–1pm, 2.45–5.15pm; Fri– Sat 10.30am–1pm; free), its *Moderniste* façade complemented by that of the bank on the oppposite corner; both were the work of Joan Rubió, who was strongly influenced by Gaudí. The church, in fact, dates from the 13th century although the main structure is 17th-century baroque. In Carrer Sa Lluna is another, more restrained, example of *Modernisme*: **Can Prunera**, dating from 1911. The town **Museum** (open Mon–Fri 11am–1pm, 5–8pm; entrance fee), at Carrer Sa Mar 13, features a collection of various local artefacts from farming equipment to ceramics and paintings.

Leave the central square by Carrer Bauza (sign to Port); after some 30m (100ft) go right then left into Carrer Cuadrado. After a few minutes you arrive at a pair of large stone posts with the inscription 'Villa Palmera'. Through the gate is the **Jardí Botanic de Sóller** i **Museu de Cièncias Naturales** (open Tues–Sat 10am–6pm, Sun 10am–2pm; entrance fee) in an early 20th-century manor (entrance around the corner on the main road). The gardens display flora from all over the Balearic Islands. It is an attractive spot but rather spoilt by being right next to a busy road.

Port de Sóller

Return to the town centre to catch the tramvia to Port de Sóller, either at the railway station or at the corner of the main square and Carrer Cristobal Colóm. Trams run every half hour between 7am and 8.15pm, stopping en route where requested, and the journey takes about 20 minutes. The open-air wagons run behind some of the village houses, giving you a closer look at the small gardens which adjoin virtually every house in Sóller. You pass through orange and lemon groves and then travel parallel to the main road before entering the port.

The tram stops every 100m (110yds) or so along the water's edge, so get off when you like. If you get off at the first stop, next to the **Plaça de la Torre**, you can hike around the beach, along the **Passeig de la Platja**, eventually arriving at the lighthouse. Continuing to the last stop, will bring you to the middle of the port. Beyond the station is the public wharf, crowded with boats which cruise (in summer only) to **Sa Calobra**, **Na Foradada** and the **Formentor Peninsula**.

On the hill abovethe port is the church of **Santa Catalina** and a lookout point giving a view over the coast to the north. Further up the hill is the **Torre Picada**, an ancient watchtower. If you are looking for somewhere to eat, there are several seafood restaurants on Carrer Santa Catalina at the bottom of the hill.

12. WINDMILLS OF THE PLA DE PALMA *(see map, p43)*

A drive through Mallorca's windmill country, followed by a windswept cape, a prehistoric site, and one of the island's most beautiful beaches.

One of the images associated with Mallorca is that of a windmill silhou-etted against mountains. To get to the Pla de Palma, where the majority of the island's windmills are, leave Palma by following signs to Mana-cor. After the village of **Son Ferriol** you enter open farm country. The windmills are in various states of repair. Some are in total decay, others recently abandoned, while some have been restored and are turning in the wind, while yet others have become restaurants and artisan centres. Their

original purpose was to suck the marshland dry for farming.

A short distance past the vil-lage of Sa Casa Blanca, you arrive at a junction flanked by two restaurants, Es Control and Punta Son Gual. Turn right and follow the road signposted to the airport and Platja de Palma. On the left you pass the village of **Sant Jordi** and alongside the air-port runway. From here follow the signs to Santanyí, on the PM-19 highway. Continue past exits 3 and 4, and turn off at exit 5 in the direction of Cala Blava.

At the next roundabout you will be near **Aquacity** *(see page 81)*, with its tow-ering water ramps. Go straight on to the next roundabout The PMV-6014 is lined with holiday developments; after a while they peter out, and you enter an open landscape, the driest part of the island. When the **Cap Blanc** lighthouse comes into view at around Km17, you are getting close to the 150-m/492-ft cliff edge. Since the lighthouse is inhabited, skirt the compound to the right to enjoy the view back towards the Badia de Palma.

Continuing along the road in front of the military encampment you drive into the harshest region of Mallorca. Until very recently, the land here was used for little else than grazing sheep and hunting. The Talayotic village of **Capocorb Vell** (open Fri–Wed 10am–5pm; entrance fee), dating from 1000BC, is found on a sharp right-hand curve. The complex, the largest of its type on Mallorca, contains five *talayots* and 28 dwellings.

Ater another 7km (4 miles), you will come to a crossroads with a sign for S'Estanyol to the right along the PMV-6015. **S'Estanyol** and its neigh-bouring village, **Sa Ràpita**, are growing at a rapid pace as Mallorcans from the capital build summer homes. Both centres have their own yacht clubs.

White Sands and Clear Water

About 1km (½ mile) after the La Rápita Yacht Club, turn right at a sign indicating **Ses Covetes** and follow the secondary road to the village. As the entrance to Mallorca's most famous beach, **Es Trenc**, the village becomes

Above: windmill in Mallorcan national colours

ensnarled with traffic every weekend. The beach, which runs for around 4 km (2½ miles), is beautiful and great for swimming but often crowded. There is, however, a wide swathe of dunes and pine trees behind the fine white sands. Out to sea is the little island of Cabrera.

It is also possible to access Es Trenc from the southern end: from Colònia de Sant Jordi take the turning to Campos, and a further 3km (2 miles) look for the sign to the beach. From here it is a few more kilometres across the salt pans of the **Salinas de Levant** (excellent for birdwatching) to the car park and the beach. Leave Ses Covetes and turn right at the first possible turn off, left at the next and then right at the main road (PMV-6014), where you find signs reading Palma/Campos. Two kilometres (1¼ miles) further on, turn south towards **Colòni de Sant Jordi**. Until a few years ago *Sa Coloni* was an attractive little seaside village, but it has grown rapidly with a great deal of ugly development. Nevertheless, the restaurant **La Lonja**, on the fishermen's quay, is one of many here that make a good place for lunch, and the beach to the left of the town beach is a pleasant spot for a swim. There are excursions from the port (Apr–Oct: daily) to the uninhabited island of **Cabrera**, used as a prison during the Napoleonic Wars. Thousands of French soldiers starved to death here between 1809 and 1813. There is a memorial on the island, which is today part o fa nature reserve.

Return to Palma by way of Campos and Llucmajor. If you go through Campos's main street, stop at the **Pastelería Pomar** (on the right just past the parish church), which is reputed to have the best pastries on the island.

13. SERRA DE TRAMUNTANA FOOTHILLS *(see map, p40–41)*

A tour of this beautiful but relatively unknown region, visiting the bucolic Vall d'Orient and the dramatic ruins of the Castell d'Alaro.

Probably the least known region of Mallorca is the area of the **Serra de Tramuntana** foothills. To explore this fascinating region, leave Palma by way of Carrer 31 de Desembre, which becomes the C-711 once past the city limits. Follow the signs towards Sóller, passing on the left the dormitory village of Palmanyola.

At Km14, turn right towards **Bunyola** and follow the road upwards till it crosses the Palma–Sóller railway tracks. At the stop sign, look directly to your left into the orchards where you will see, about 500m/yds away, the tiled yellow spire of a house called **Villa Francisca**, which is one of the few intact examples of *Modernisme* on the island, outside Palma and Sóller. The village is known for its wine, excellent olive oil and herbal liqueurs.

Right: Villa Francisca, Bunyola

Leave the village by way of a left turn at the square onto Carrer Major, climbing up through the village towards the mountains and highway PM-210, past stone walls and 500-year-old olive trees. On the left-hand side of the road is the majestic **Serra d'Alfàbia**. After passing over the *coll* (pass) you see, on the descent, the fields of the **Vall d'Orient**, with the arched balcony of Son Perot *possessió* almost centred in the valley, known as the Valley of the Apples for its many fruit orchards.

Orient and Castell d'Alaro

The sleepy village of Orient, the highest point of which stands at 455m (1,493ft), sits at the eastern end of the valley. The Església de Sant Jordi is in 16th- and 17th-century style, and it has a large ceramic panel showing Sant Jordi (St George – the patron saint of the village) killing the dragon. The house called Cal Rei dates from 1644. People come from all over the island to eat here. If price is no consideration, Hotel L'Hermitage, 5 minutes' drive east of the village (Carretera Alaró-Bunyola, tel: 971 180 303), is an ideal place for lunch; or try the suckling pig at the cheaper Restaurant Orient in town.

Continuing in the direction of Alaró, you can see, to the left at Km14, the *possessió* of **Sollerich**, once well known for its olives and olive oil. As the road descends it runs between two table-top mountains. To the left is the mountain of **S'Alcadena** and, to the right, the **Puig d'Alaró**, on top of which sits the ruins of the **Castell d'Alaró**, famous for holding out against the Aragónese invasion of 1285. The turning for the castle is at Km18, but the road does not go all the way up – it's about an hour's walk from **Es Verger** restaurant or 40 minutes' from the Bar Es Pouet (it is possible to drive further but only with a four-wheel-drive vehicle). The energetic can also walk up from Orient.

The Castell d'Alaró is one of Mallorca's three 'rock castles'. Chosen because of obvious ease of fortification and its commanding views, this site has been used for defence since for more than 2,000 years ago. The ruined structure itself dates from Moorish times, although it was rebuilt by Jaume I after the Reconquest. Following the Aragónese invasion of 1285, the castle held out for four years; after it capitulated, Alfonso III had the two commanders roasted alive for their defiance.

At the summit (822m/2,696ft), apart from the ruins there is a bar serving simple meals, a small hostel (tel: 971 510 480), a chapel and stunning views extending over most of the island.

Above: typically narrow alleyway, Orient
Right: view of the Puig d'Alaró

Alaró is a maze of one-way streets and cul-de-sacs. The oldest part, around the **Plaça de l'Ajuntament** (Town Hall Square), may be worth a walk around, but it is much like other towns along the route. The exit from the village is via Carrer Manyoles, in the direction of Inca and Lloseta. When you reach the crossroads, follow the signs to the left towards Lloseta (2km/1¼ miles).

Lloseta and Biniamar

Upon entering **Lloseta** (pronounced *Yo-seta*), continue into the centre and the **Plaça d'Espanya**. Next to the parish church is **Can Ayamans**, a large rose-coloured building with gardens open to the public on summer Saturday and Sunday afternoons. Afterwards, continue along Carrer Joan Carles I, which eventually takes you out of the village in the direction of **Biniamar**, one of dozens of sleepy little towns in Mallorca that have been overlooked by the tourist industry. Apart from the interesting stone architecture around the **Plaça de sa Quintana**, the highlight of the village is a roofless church, the interior of which is now used as a football field.

The PMV-2113 continues past groves and orchards of almond, olive, carob and fig trees, always with the mountain range on the left. As you turn left at the crossroads for the next village, the highway turns into the PMV-2112 and enters **Mancor de la Vall**. One of the focal points of this community is the 'typical' restaurant of **Turixant**. Another is the *possessió* of **Massanella**.

Caimari, the next mountain village along the route, has two churches of interest. One is the church of the **Placeta Vella** with its Renaissance entranceway. The other is the parish church, situated on the edge of the **Plaça Major**.

Turning south in the direction of Inca and Selva, you are treated to a spectacular view in your rear view mirror — Caimari nestled against the mountains. To explore **Selva** turn right in the town centre. A walk along Carrer Angels to Jaume Estelrich affords an overview of much of Mallorca. A street called **Aires de Muntanya** provides a finishing touch to this route.

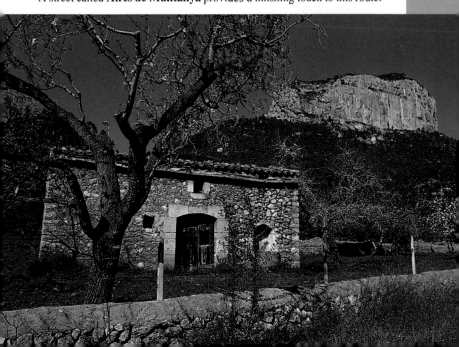

14. NORTHWEST OF PALMA　*(see map, p33)*

A tour of the area to the northwest of Palma, visiting the country estate of Sa Granja and the mountain village of Galilea.

Take the Esporles road from Palma. After a few kilometres the road climbs to reveal a panorama of the Vall de Esporles, and then snakes downhill before entering **Esporles** through a long avenue of sycamore trees. The first part of Esporles, new town, or Vilanova, was built at the beginning of the 20th century when the village was heavily dependent on the local textile industry. The oldest part of town is centred on the parish church, the **Església de Sant Pere Apòstol**, which is also on the main street near the **Plaça d'Espanya**. On the other side of the **Torrent de Sant Pere** some of the streets still retain much of their original Mallorcan character.

A Country Estate

From Esporles it is just a short drive to the estate of **Sa Granja** (open May–Oct: daily 10am–7pm; Nov–Apr: 10am– 6pm; entrance fee). The site has been known for its abundant supply of spring water since Roman times. It was of considerable importance to the Moors, who called it 'Alpich'. After the Christian invasion of 1229 the estate passed into the hands of the Cistercians, who used the fertile land to grow fruit and vegetables – hence the name (a *granja* is a farm). It was later sold, and by the late 1600s was owned by the Fortuny family who reconstructed the property in the form seen today, contributing the Italian-style *loggia* and the gardens. The Fortuny's remained until 1985, when Sa Granja was sold to the present owner. The property maintains much of its original layout, with the farm chores being carried out on the lower floor, and the living quarters upstairs. The interior has been renovated as a museum of rural life in the 18th and 19th centuries. It is imaginatively done, although the torture chamber is rather

Top: inside the museum at Sa Granja
Left: a young islander poses

unpleasant. You can wander through the wooded grounds of the estate. Things are further enlivened (Wed and Fri 3.30–5pm) by demonstrations of traditional handicrafts and regional music and folk dancing, and there are always tastings of locally-made fig bread, cheese and sausages.

Leave by way of the PMV-1101 (to Puigpunyent), through the **Vall de Superna**. The narrow, winding road passes through a typical Mallorcan forest of pine and holm oak *(encina)*. Here you get your first look at the rocky mass of Galatzó before descending to the village of **Puigpunyent**. Son Net, an exclusive hotel occupying a country manor just outside the village, has an excellent (but expensive) restaurant.

A possible excursion from Puigpunyent leads west to **La Reserva de Puig de Galatzó** (open Apr–Oct: daily 10am–7pm; Nov–Mar: 10am–6pm; last entrance 2 hours before closing time; entrance fee), located on the eastern flanks of Galatzó peak, at 1,026m (3,366ft) the highest mountain hereabouts. Activities here include abseiling, archery, orienteering, horse-riding and mountain biking, and there is a network of scenic hiking trails.

Galilea and Calviá

From Puigpunyent, follow signs to Es Capdellà and the PMV-1032 highway. In less than 10 minutes, you will arrive in the tiny mountain village of **Galilea**. Although the village has recently been the site of some uncontrolled building, the area around the tiny baroque church has kept its charm. In the **Plaça del Papa Pio XII** (next to the church) you can lunch with an excellent view as far as the sea. The restaurant here, with outdoor tables, has some interesting Mallorcan desserts.

On the winding road down to **Es Capdellà** you are treated, from time to time, to views out over the Costa de Calviá. Proceed to **Calviá**, the administrative centre of the area. Approaching the village, a large sports complex is the introduction to the recent building boom here, as is a similarly oversized town hall in the centre. Calviá is rumoured to be the richest municipality in Spain. **Sant Joan Bautista** parish church, flanking the central square, was built in the last decade of the 19th century. A hermitage of the same name lies outside the town. On the façade of the old town hall there is a large ceramic plaque depicting 700 years of the history of the village.

If you're still game for a little more sightseeing, continue through Calviá along Carrer Major till it rejoins the PMV-1034 towards Establiments. The road winds through a part of Mallorca which has changed little for hundreds of years. After Km7, turn right onto a secondary road which soon climbs into forested hills. With spectacular views of the Badia de Palma (Palma Bay) and the Castell de Bellver, the road soon reaches the city's outskirts. Going straight over two roundabouts you will pass the social security hospital of Son Dureta and enter town via Carrer Andrea Doria.

Right: garden statue at Sa Granja

15. AROUND ALCUDIA BAY *(see maps, p40–41 and 63)*

Starting at the walled town of Alcúdia with its Roman ruins, visit the wetland nature reserve of Parc Natural S'Albufera and the old towns of Artà and Capdepera.

The strategically-located city of **Alcúdia** was built on the site of Roman Pollentia, which in turn lay over the site of an earlier Phoenician town. It later became an important Moorish settlement (Al-Kudia means 'on the hill'). The impressive restored walls were originally constructed in the 14th and 16th centuries; those standing today escaped demolition when the parish church of Sant Jaume was erected in 1893.

The approach from Palma brings you along the Avinguda d'Inca; turn right at the roundabout next to the walls (signposted to Port d'Alcúdia), follow the

road around the left hand bend, and you will come to a car park next to the walls on the left. Enter through the walls into the Plaça de Jaume Oués Prevere beside the parish church of **Sant Jaume**. Within the church – most of its structure dates from the late 19th century – is the Capella del Sant Cristo, built in 1697. Adjoining it is the **Museu Parroquial** (open Tues–Fri 10am–1pm, Sun 10am–noon; entrance fee) containing an interesting collection of religious relics and paintings dating back many centuries.

Past the church to the left is the **Museu Monogràfic de Pollentia** (open Tues–Fri 10am–1.15pm, 3.30–5.15pm, Sat–Sun 10.30am–12.45pm; entrance fee includes Ciutat Romana but either can be visited separately)

Top: Roman ruins at the Teatre Romà, Alcúdia
Above: fishing on the beach

which holds a small collection of Roman finds from all over Mallorca. At the end of Carrer Sant Jaume is the old palace of **Can Torró**, now a public library. There are some pleasant cafés and restaurants on the central **Plaça Constitució**, and a lively Sunday market is held just outside the town walls.

The remains of one of the island's oldest archaeological sites, the **Ciutat Romana del Pollentia** (open Tues–Fri 10am–3.30pm, Sat–Sun 10.30am–1.30pm; entrance fee) also stand outside the walls. The ruins, which are rather sparse, are only part of the settlement founded by the Roman consul Quinto Cecilio Metelo, after the conquest of Mallorca in 123BC. Excavated in the 1950s by members of a dig organised by American archaeologist, William Bryant, the area includes remnants of two buildings, and gives an idea of the town's layout. The **Teatre Romà** (open access; free), which also dates from the 2nd century BC, lies further down the road to Port d'Alcúdia, where there is a sign to the right. The remains of a semi-circular stage and tiers are still visible, and the acoustics are excellent.

Returning in the direction of Alcúdia, turn right at the traffic lights and follow the signs towards Mal Pas on the way to the hermitage, the **Ermita de la Victòria**. The road winds along the rocky coastline, past the small resort at Bonaire and through pine woods full of picnickers at weekends. Eventually it leads to the 17th-century hermitage church and the restaurant **Mirador**, a good place to stop for lunch. From here a path leads up to the watchtower of **Atalaia d'Alcúdia**, dating from 1567, part of a string of defensive towers that once lined the coast.

Retrace your route pass the Teatre Romà, and head for **Port d'Alcúdia.** This big, brash resort is almost entirely a new creation, built around a small fishing harbour and consisting of hundreds of souvenir shops, cafeterias, hotels, apartments and discos, plus a very well-kept beach. You can get a ferry to Menorca from the port. To the inland side of this development, sits the **Puig de Sant Martí**, Mallorca's number one hang-gliding peak.

A Haven for Wildlife
Follow the signs to Can Picafort, and about 5km (3 miles) along the coastal road you will find, on the right, the entrance to the **Parc Natural S'Albufera** (open Apr–Sept: daily 9am–6pm; Oct–Mar 9am–5pm; free), a marshland preserve well known to ornithologists and conservationists all over Europe. At the end of a gravel path is a helpful orientation centre from which one

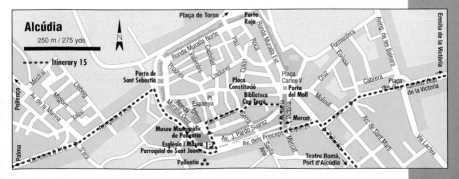

must pick up a permit before striking out on nature walks or watching a variety of water birds from well-appointed hides. A visit is particularly rewarding during the spring and autumn migrations, when tens of thousands of birds stop here en route to northern Europe or Africa. With a bit of luck you may also sse the herd of water buffalo, imported to eat the canal weeds.

The C-712, now in the county of Muro, passes through the extensive strip of **Can Picafort** and later twists between the *possessió* of Son Serra de Marina and a small church, the Oratori de Sant Joan. The road cuts though pine forests and offers a fine view of the fortress-like mountain of Ferrutx, its neighbour, Morey, and the high headland of Sa Talaia Moreia, before it passes the road for **Colònia de Sant Pere**, a small-scale resort with an impressive mountain backdrop, on the south side of the Badia d'Alcúdia. The coast in this part of Mallorca remains largely undeveloped due to its lack of sandy beaches.

Artà and Betlem

Enter **Artà** by Carrer Sant Margalida, and make your way to the highest point of town. The Via Crucis, a broad flight of steps lined with cypresses, leads up from the parish church of the **Transfiguració del Senyor** to the **Santuari de Sant Salvador**, a great fortress begun in the 13th century on the site of the Arabic *almudaina*. You can walk along the battlemented walls for splendid views of the town and the plain spread out below. The **Museu Regional d'Artà** (open Mon–Fri 10am–1pm; entrance fee) on the Plaça d'Espanya in the centre of town displays Phoenician, Greek and Roman relics and has a natural science collection.

The area around Artà is rich in archaeological remains, the most important being the Talayotic village of **Ses Païsses** (open Apr–Sept: daily 9am–1pm, 3–7pm; Oct–Mar: Mon–Sat 9am–1pm, 2.30–5pm; entrance fee), south of Artà and signposted off the Capdepera road. A rewarding side trip is to the isolated **Ermita de Betlem**, 10km (6 miles) to the north (leave Artà beside the path to the sanctuary). It takes at least an hour along the narrowPMV-3333. About halfway along you will see the fortified medieval tower of **Son Morei Vell**. At the hermitage, which is largely in ruins, climb to the hilltop for a spectacular view across the Badia d'Alcúdia.

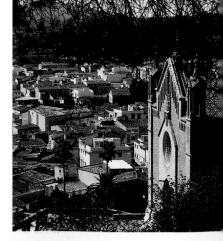

Top: hoopoes are common in S'Albufera
Right: overview of Artà

16. THE NORTHEAST COAST *(see map, p66)*

Explore the caves and coves of Mallorca's easternmost corner, visit a private garden with Henry Moore sculptures, a medieval castle and watchtower, and Europe's largest underground lake.

Start the tour at Mallorca's most easterly tip, the resort town of **Cala Ratjada**. The **Jardins Casa March**, on a hill above the harbour, are home to a collection of contemporary sculpture, including works by Auguste Rodin, Henry Moore and Eduardo Chillida. The grounds are open by arrangment only; contact the Tourist Office in the **Plaça dels Pins** (tel: 971 563 033). If you have time, it is a visit worth planning. The resort itself is busy and somewhat over-commercialised, but much of the seafront is very pleasant. Take a stroll through the pine forest to the **Far de Capdepera** (lighthouse), with views across to Menorca. There are fine beaches at Cala Agulla just to the north of the town, and at Cala Mesquida on the other side of the Cap des Freu (reached by road from Capdepera), as well as at Son Moll to the south. In summer there are boat trips to the Coves d'Artà *(see page 66)*.

Castles and Caves

Capdepera is a short drive inland. The main sight here is the large hilltop fortress, visible for miles around. Turning right onto Carrer de's Collegi, you eventually pass the **Plaça de l'Orient**. If you want to climb to the fortress, this is a good place to leave your car. Turn right and climb up the steps of **Es Pla de'n Cosset**. To go by car, continue two more blocks to Carrer Major and turn right.

The **Castell de Capdepera** (open Apr–Oct: daily 10am–8pm; Nov–Mar: 10am–5pm; entrance fee), the largest on the island, was begun by the Romans, enlarged by the Moors and fortified further by the Christians. Within its massive walls is the Gothic **Capella de Nostra Senyora de la Esperança**, the earliest mention of which dates back to the times of the Catalan con-

Above: summer time at Port d'Alcúdia

quest in the 13th century. It is situated on the spot where King Jaume I accepted the surrender of the Moors in 1231.

To leave the village, turn right on Carrer Gómez Ulla and follow signs for Son Servera. After 3km (2 miles) take a left turn signposted to the Coves d'Artà, which is quickly followed by another left turn onto the PMV-4042. Continue past the Canyamel golf course and the megalithic site of **Es Claper des Gegant**, and follow more signs to the **Coves d'Artà** (open Apr–Sept: daily 10am–7pm, Oct–Mar: 10am–5pm; entrance fee), at the end of the clifftop road. Carved out of the sheer cliff face, these are perhaps the most spectacular caves on the island and they have a grisly history; 2,000 Moors hid in the caves after Jaume I's invasion of the island, and the Catalan troops smoked them out then slaughtered every one. Visitors are permitted to take pictures during the half-hour long tour.

The beach, the **Platja de Canyamel**, is reached by a flight of steps from the car park near the cave entrance. The only way to get there is to walk. The **Hostal Cuevas** makes a good stop for lunch.

To get to the **Torre de Canyamel**, return past the golf course and make two left turns, following signs to Canyamel. The medieval watchtower and museum are open to visitors. The key can be obtained in the restaurant, which is closed Sunday afternoon and all day Monday.

When you arrive back at the PM-404, turn south towards Son Servera, bypassing the long strip of development around the beach resorts of Cala Bona, Cala Millor, Sa Coma and S'Illot, which fuse into one another along the coast. Follow the signs for Porto Cristo, and you will

come to **Safari Zoo** (open Apr–Sept: daily 9am–7pm; Oct–Mar: 9am–5pm; entrance fee; tel: 971 810 909), on the right just after the turn-off for Sa Coma. A wide variety of animals can be observed from a mini-train, or from your own car.

Along the East Coast

Porto Cristo, the port of the town of Manacor, is best known as the home of the Coves del Drac and the Coves dels Hams. In 1936 the town saw Mallorca's only action of the Spanish Civil War, when a Republican battleship landed here with a force of 12,000. The troops managed to advance 10km (6 miles) from here, but the Nationalists soon drove them back. It's a pleasant, rather old-fahioned resort, with a huge yacht harbour. The area around the port is quite lively. Take a stroll down the slope of Carrer Burdils, which parallels the beach, and down the steps to the fishermen's quay, following the edge of the inlet as it snakes into town. The church of **Nostra Senyora del Carme** in the square on Carrer Çanglada is interesting.

The **Coves del Drach** (open Apr–Oct: daily 10am–5pm; Nov–Mar: 10.45am–3.30pm; entrance fee) to the south of town, are Porto Cristo's main attraction. Regular tours, ending with a musical performance, run through the brightly-lit 2km (1 mile) of chambers and spectacular rock formations. The highlight is the 177-m (581-ft) long subterranean lake named after Edouard-Alfred Martel, the French speleologist who explored the caves in 1896. Jules Verne is said to have been inspired by a visit to write *Journey to the Centre of the Earth*. Alternatively you can visit the **Coves dels Hams** (open Apr–Sept: daily 10am–6pm; Oct–Mar: 10.30am–5pm; entrance fee), about 1km (½ mile) out of town, which were discovered in 1905. Again, there is a subterranean lake and musical performances.

The road leads south through pine woods to **Porto Colom**. The port area is reached by turning left by an old anchor as you enter, skirting the bay beside Passeig Miquel Massuti. The port was the export centre for local wines, a profitable business until the outbreak of *phylloxera* in 1870. Local history is reflected in its street names – Mar, Ancora and Vela (Sea, Anchor and Sail) – as well as the row of waterside boat sheds running alongside **Es Riuetó**.

Cuevas del Drach

Top: family photo at Cala Millor
Right: Porto Cristo's main attraction

17. SOUTHEAST MALLORCA *(see map, p66)*

Visit the impressive hilltop sanctuaries of this corner of the island, and the coast at the picturesque cove of Cala Figuera.

Leave Palma by the airport highway and follow the signs to Felanitx, through Llucmajor and Campos. **Felanitx** is a town with the reputation of producing the best brains in Mallorca. A number of politicians, writers, architects and intellectuals are proud Felanitxers, as is the acclaimed contemporary artist, Miquel Barceló. The town is a good place to buy ceramics; and the church of **Sant Miquel** has one of the best baroque façades on the island.

Hilltop Retreats

Follow the signs to Sant Salvador/Porto Colom. A couple of kilometres out of town you will be greeted by two neat stone pillars, on top of which are small crosses. Turn right onto the secondary pmv-4011 and drive to the Santuari de Sant Salvador, Mallorca's most impressive hilltop hermitage, rewards visitors with a stunning panorama from its dramatic position atop a 509m (1,670ft) mountain. The enormous stone cross on one side of the hill is visible from miles around; on the other side is the monument to Cristo Rei (both 20th century). The original church here was built in 1348, but after a second was added at the end of the 16th century the site was largely destroyed by marauding pirates; most of the present structure is 18th century. The alabaster retable in the church dates from around 1500, and shows details of the Passion and Last Supper. There is a restaurant, and it is possible to rent rooms here (tel: 971 827 282).

To reach the **Castell de Santueri** (open Apr–Oct: daily 10am–7pm) you must return to Felanitx, then head south on the Calonge road. A left turn leads up to the site. This is one of only three 'rock castles' (fortified hilltops) on

Mallorca, the others being at Alaró and Pollença. The site is likely to have been used as far back as Roman times, and there are ruins from virtually every period of Mallorca's past, each element being used or discarded by the subsequent occupying power.

Continue south towards Calonge, then follow the road for Alqueria Blanca and Santanyi (both have a number of handicrafts shops). Just past Alqueria Blanca is a right turn to the **Oratori de Nostra Senyora de la Consolació**. This is one of the best-kept examples of 17th-century Mallorcan architecture on the island. Today the building is cared for by the families of the *Amics del Santuari*, who are responsible for open-

Left: Santuari de Sant Salvador

ing the site every day of the year. The age of the oratory is attested to by a date, 1677, on the patio wall and another of 1646 on a wooden altarpiece.

Santanyi and the Coast

Santanyí has something most other places in Mallorca would like – honey-coloured sandstone which, besides being extremely attractive, is also very durable. Consequently, the town is in a much better state of repair than most of its neighbours. The stone has been well known since the Middle Ages, when it was chosen as the building material for such edifces as Sa Llotja in Palma and the Castellnovo in Naples. The houses' distinguishing feature is a stone supporting the windowsills above the arched doorways. The huge parish church of Sant Andreu Apostel dominates the elongated Plaça Major. Arty little Santanyí has several exhibition venues and a number of antique and ceramics shops.

It is a short distance to the picturesque harbour of **Cala Figuera**, with whitewashed cottages and boathouses along the water's edge, and some good seafood restaurants. This is a popular resort that has managed to retain its charm, partly because it has no sandy beach – the nearest beach is at Cala Santanyi, about 3km (2 miles) down the coast. Just to the south is an attractive beach at **Cala Llombards**. To the north of Cala Figuera, near the tiny resort and bay of **Cala Mondragó**, the wetlands of the **Parc Natural de Mondragó** (information office open daily 9am–4pm) provide excellent birdwatching opportunities and good walks through the protected parkland.

Top: Sant Salvador has a commanding view over the plain
Right: the beaches along the east coast are popular with families

shopping

Leisure
Activities

SHOPPING

For centuries, Mallorca has been a centre of Mediterranean trade and has fostered a range of artistic and industrial activities that have created a substantial reputation for the island, both at home and abroad.

Glassmaking

Mallorca has a long tradition of glassmaking, and there are two glass-blowing factories that can be visited on the island: **Lafiore**, at S'Esgleieta 7km (4 miles) from Valldemossa, and **Vidriera Gordiola** *(see page 43)*, which is just before Algaida on the busy Palma–Manacor road. The latter glassworks also has two shops in **Palma** – one at Carrer Jaume II 14, and another at Carrer Victória 2.

Pottery and Ceramics

Although many towns in Mallorca have a tradition of making pottery and ceramics, it is the village of **Pòrtol**, a short distance northeast of Palma, which has the most working kilns. As well as the typical red, white and green clay-figure whistles called *siurells,* which are said to have originated in Muslim times, you will find lots of other ceramic items, including the heavy, brown cooking pots – *ollas.* Roca Llisa in Carrer Roca Llisa is best for *siurells.* Ca'n Vent and Ca's Canonge, both in Carrer Trinitat, are good for kitchen ceramics. In Palma, two places to shop for ceramics are **Fet a Má** at Carrer Sant Miquel 52 (also good for glass), and **Fang i Foc** at Carrer Libertat 29.

Textiles

The most popular product is the cloth known as **roba de llengües** ('cloth of tongues', pronounced *yengos*), named for the colourful, tongue-shaped patterns that are stamped on the woven cotton. It continues to be made

in Inca, Santa Maria and Pollença as well as in the capital. One of the most traditional shops in the trade is **Herederos de Vicente Juan Ribas** at Carrer Sant Nicolau 10, in Palma, just up the hill from the church.

Bordados (crochet) is another speciality of Mallorcan traditional crafts. **Casa Bonet** at Plaça Frédéric Chopin 2, in Palma, is renowned for the work. Always look for the label *Hecho a mano* or *Fet a má* to ensure items are handmade.

Woodcarving

The decline in Mallorca's olive oil industry has given rise to the use of olive wood for decorative purposes. **La Casa del Olivo**, at Carrer Pescatería Vella 4, Palma, sells beautiful olive-wood salad bowls and other items. You pay for the craftmanship. At Carretera Palma–Manacor Km 45, **OlivArt** is another place worth checking out

Leather

The manufacture of leather goods and shoes is one of the most important industrial activities on the island. **Inca** is the home of most of the better-known brands and, as well as factory outlets, you can visit the factories themselves *(see page 34).* When buying from

Left: Sunday market stalls at Artà
Right: *ensaimadas,* sweet Mallorcan pastries, come in various sizes

Rei Joan Carles I. The main Perlas Majorica outlet is at Avinguda Jaume III 11.

Wine and Liqueurs

Vineyards are found in the central area of Mallorca around Binissalem–Consell–Santa Maria, and in the southeast around Felanitx. Among wines that can be recommended are those produced in Binissalem by **Franja Roja** (mostly *tintos* – reds) and **Bodega Antonio Nadal** (*tinto* and *blanco*) and those of **Herederos de Hermanos Ribas** from Consell, who also produce a decent *rosé*.

Mallorca is known for its herbal **liqueurs**. The most popular aperitif, **Palo Tunel**, made in Bunyola, comes in both sweet *(dulce)* and dry *(amargo)* varieties. **Hierbas**, is drunk after a meal as a *digestivo*. In Palma, try buying them in **La Vinoteca** at Plaça Mare de Déu de la Salut 3 (off Carrer Sant Miquel), or **Llofriu**, Carrer Sant Nicolau 23.

Pastries and Other Delights

Mallorcan *dulces* or sweets are a speciality, and there is a great variety. The most popular of all is the delectable *ensaimada*. This is a soft, fluffy pastry made from wheat flour, lard and water and dusted with sugar. Circular in shape, it is sold plain or with various fillings. *Ensaimadas* , which originated in Menorca, are sold in almost every bakery on the island, in individual sizes, such as are often eaten for breakfast, or in family sizes, packaged in appropriately large, round boxes for export (you will see them in the departure lounge at the airport when you leave). **Forn Fondo** at Carrer Unió 15 and the ornate, *Moderniste* **Forn des Teatre** at Plaça Weyler 9, are good places to buy in Palma; as is **Pastelería Pomar** at Carrer Baró de Santa Maria de Sepulcre; there is another branch in Campos. Sóller is known for its *picos de marzapan*, little white marzipan pyramids, sold in all the local bakeries.

Olive oil and olives are also good things to buy. Markets are the best places to find a variety of olives, but for oil and interesting food of all kinds, go to the old-fashioned little **Colmado Santo Domingo** in Carrer

the factory you can expect a small discount, but the days of true bargains are gone.

Two of the best-known factories in Inca are the quirky and fashionable **Camper**, whose shoes are highly individual, some painted with flowers and trees, others with left and right partners slightly different; and **Munper**, for shoes, bags ands belts. The latter also has a shop in Montuiri, and Camper shoes can be bought in Palma, at Avinguda Jaume III and elsewhere. **Passy**'s elegant shoes can also be found in Palma, also on Avinguda Jaume III. Less trendy, but extremely attractive and comfortable are *abarcas*, the slipper-like sandals made in Menorca that have been worn by peasants for centuries and now come in a range of vivid and subtle colours for around €25.

Artificial Pearls

Since the beginning of the century, when the fabrication of pearls began in Mallorca, Manacor has been the centre of the industry. As well as **Orquidea** and **Majorica**, there are various smaller companies which compete for the tourist market. Although there are many tours to Manacor that include a 5-minute run-through of the manufacturing process, we suggest you save the trip and buy the pearls from one of the outlets in Palma. The prices are very similar, and you are treated better because the shops aren't so crowded. One official Orquidea outlet is in the centre of the city on Plaça

Above: *hierbas* is enjoyed after a meal

Sant Domingo, where strings of garlic and peppers, cured hams and sausages festoon the window and the dim interior.

Antiques

There are various well-known antiques shops throughout the island, most notably in Santa Mariá, Consell, S'Alquería Blanca and Pollença. In Palma, **Antigüedades Casa Delmonte**, La Rambla (Via Roma) 8; and **Midge Dalton** at Plaça Mercat 20, are representative. The latter also has good jewellery and paintings. **Antigüedades Sa Costa** at Costa de Sa Pols 9 and **Persepolis**, at Avinguda Jaume III are two other interesting antique shops, although the latter is pretty expensive. The **Baratillo** (flea market), which takes over the Avinguda Gabriel Alomari Villalonga every Saturday morning, is also a good place to look for antiques and bric-à-brac at affordable prices. Go early.

Art

In the last 15 years there has been something of an artistic renaissance on Mallorca. Pollença and Alcúdia both have galleries that exhibit local and foreign work. The gallery **Centre d'Art S'Estació**, in the abandoned railway station at Sineu, specialises in the work of contemporary artists. Palma has numerous galleries and, because the city is small, they can all be reached without too much difficulty. Some of the most notable venues are the **Galería Altair** at Carrer Sant Jaume 23; **Centro Pelaires** on Carrer Verí 3; **Ferrán Cano**, Carrer Font de la Glòria 12; and **Jaime III**, Avinguda Jaime III 25, which are all worth a look.

Palma also has various cultural centres that hold exhibitions on a regular basis.

Shopping in Palma

For the shopper, the relatively small size of Palma is a great advantage. **Avinguda Jaime III** (not to be confused with the small pedestrianised Carrer Jaime II, also a shopping thoroughfare) is one of Palma's most elegant avenues, lined with upmarket and more down-to-earth shops offering men's and women's fashions as well as jewellery and gifts. **El Corte Inglés**, Spain's biggest department store chain, at No 15, has a supermarket in the basement (there is another branch at Avinguda Alexandre Rosseló 12–16). For a thorough shopping spree don't forget the side streets of **Bonaire**, **Santa Maria del Sepulcro**, **Sant Martí**, etc.

Follow the broad avenue down its gentle slope to the **Plaça Rei Joan Carles I**, and the large **C&A** department store. The **Passeig del Born** has an interesting variety of shops ranging from the high-quality leather luggage and accessories of **Loewe** (which also has a branch in Avinguda Jaume III) and high-street fashion for men, women and children at **Zara**, further down on the right, to the old-fashioned, family-run **Cesteria el Centro**, which makes straw baskets, sun hats and espadrilles.

Returning to the Plaça Rei Joan Carles I again, turn right down **Carrer Brondo** to **Carrer Paraires**, on which you will find **Librería Ereso**, one of the best bookshops in the city, on the corner of **Carrer Sant Nicolau**, which is named after the church nearby. This street, along with the areas around **Plaça Chopin** and **Carrer Tous i Maroto**, forms one of the busiest commercial districts of the city. Nearby are the chic boutiques and jewellers of **Carrer Verí**, a narrow street that is worth a stroll for its architecture, even if you are not interested in designer fashion.

The main interest of **Plaça Major** is the outdoor craft market, which is held there on Monday, Friday and Saturday morning. Go straight ahead onto **Carrer Sant Miquel** or take the right-hand exit and join **Carrer Sindicat** with its seemingly never-ending line of shoe shops.

On Sant Miquel, at No 43, is **Alpargateria Llinás**, which sells rope-soled shoes and shopping bags. The street leads to **Carrer des Oms (Olmos)**. The descent on the pedestrianised street is between book and poster shops, opticians and photocopying stores. The bottom of the street again joins La Rambla after a few minutes' walk.

EATING OUT

There's a huge variety of restaurants in Mallorca, from the traditional *cellers (see page 77)* to the smart, innovative places with top-notch chefs popping up not just in Palma but all over the island. Away from the fast-food and bland 'international-style' meals on offer in the bigger resorts, you should eat well wherever you go. *Cuina mallorquina* (Mallorcan cuisine) reaches its height in the *cellers* but can be found in many other places, too. It is based on local ingredients and served in substantial helpings. Pork, in various guises, plays an important role.

For centuries, pork has been the cornerstone of the islanders' diet. Every family,, no matter how poor, fattened a pig every year and, after the *matança* (slaughter), filled the larder with sausages and chops. Also from the pig, they derived the lard which was the foundation of many dishes, both sweet and savoury.

Pork is the basis of the *sobrasada, butifarró, blanquet* and *camaiot* sausages that one sees hanging from the rafters of restaurants and delicatessens. Popular pork dishes are *llomb amb col* (pork rolled in cabbage leaves and baked); and *arròs brut* (rice with pork or sometimes chicken). *Lechona asada* (roast suckling pig) is really a Christmas dish but may be found on menus at other times.

A rich variety of vegetables are also integral to island cooking – among them aubergines, spinach and large, juicy tomatoes. In summer, dishes such as *trempó,* a salad of tomatoes, onion and green peppers is popular; and *tumbet,* aubergines, potatoes and sweet red peppers covered in tomato sauce and beaten egg and oven-baked, is a great favourite, as are *aubergines farcides,* aubergines filled with minced meat and tomato sauce.

Sopas mallorquinas – invariably referred to in this plural form – are ubiquitous. They are soups made of seasonal vegetables and poured over *pa pagès* (country bread sliced extremely thin). An interesting variety is the *sopes de matances,* which includes small pieces of pork and *setas* (a type of mushroom). Also traditional, is *frit mallorquin.* This mixture of fried potatoes, blood sausage and strips of liver, dripping in oil, is an acquired taste.

Although there are as many fish dishes as there are varieties of fish, two especially worth trying are *anfós al forn* (baked sea bass) and *caldereta de peix* (spiced fish stew, a version of *bouillabaisse*). *Caldereta de llagosta,* a Menorcan speciality, may also be found. This is a delicious, rich, lobster stew, and very expensive. Another interesting dish is fish baked in a thick coat of sea salt. It preserves the flavour but, surprisingly, does not make

Above: a table with a view

the fish taste too salty. Also notable, but not strictly a Mallorcan dish, is *calamars farcits* (stuffed squid).

Mallorca is renowned for its bread and olive oil. The bread is dense in texture, the oil thick and rich and green. So it is not surprising that *pa amb oli*, bread and oil (pronounced *pamboli*), is served everywhere. It is simply toasted bread rubbed with garlic, sprinkled with salt and lubricated with olive oil. It may also be rubbed with fresh tomatoes, when it becomes *pa amb tomàquet*.

Savoury pastries, found in bakeries (*panaderías*) or pastry shops (*pastelerías*), make popular snacks. *Empanades* are small round pies filled with meat and peas; *coca de verdura* is similar to a pizza but is rectangular in shape and eaten cold. The *cocarois* is half-moon shaped and filled with *bledes* (chard, similar to spinach).

Dolç (desserts) range from the typical *gelat de ametla* served with *coca de gató* (almond ice cream with almond cake) to large, star-shaped biscuits called *crespells* and *coca de patata* (a sweet bread that is a speciality of Valldemossa), as well as *greixonera de brossat*, a type of cheesecake. The *ensaimada*, a spiral-shaped, sugar-dusted confection may be eaten as a dessert, but is more commonly consumed with coffee at breakfast time.

As in the rest of Spain, people in Mallorca eat late. Lunch may begin between 2 and 3pm, dinner around 10pm. However, restaurateurs know that Northern Europeans like to eat earlier, and open their doors and their kitchens accordingly.

Most places offer a *menú del día* at lunchtime; although it limits your choices it is an economical way to eat, as you usually get three courses with bread and a glass of wine for a low price (typically around €10–12).

The following price guide indicates the approximate price of a three-course meal for one, with house wine, but prices do vary a great deal and this should be used only as a general guide: €€€ = €40–80, €€ = €25–40, € = under €25.

Right: salt-baked fish

Where to Eat in Palma

Aramis
Carrer Montenegro 1
Tel: 971 725 232
Minimalist, new and stylish, with modern, Italian-influenced food. Closed Sun. €€€

Bon Lloc
Carrer Sant Feliu 7
Tel: 971 718 617
Great vegetarian restaurant, with a good set menu. Lunch only. €

Caballito del Mar
Passeig Sagrera 5
Tel: 971 721 074
Well-prepared fish and shellfish dishes, just off the lively Plaça Sa Llonja. €€

Ca'n Carlos
Carrer de S'Aigua 5
Tel: 971 713 869
Authentic Mallorcan dishes in a popular, family-run restaurant. Central location. €€

Celler Sa Premsa
Plaça Bisbe Berenguer de Palou 8
Tel: 971 723 529
Traditional *bodega*; Mallorcan dishes; good seafood. Very popular. Closed Sat–Sun. €

Es Parlament
Carrer Conquistador 11
Tel: 971 726 026
Stylish setting in a classic building. Good traditional food; paella is their speciality. Closed Mon and August. €

Montenegro
Carrer Montenegro 10
Tel: 971 728 957
A varied menu is served in this newish restaurant in a converted celler. The street

offers a number of other eating opportunities, including the stylish Opio restaurant in the nearby Hotel Tres. €

Koldo Royo
Passeig Marítim (Avinguda Ingeniero Gabriel Roca) 3
Tel: 971 732 435
Cool dining room with dark mahogany furniture and white linen. Long-established and regarded as one of Palma's best restaurants. Highly-regarded Basque cuisine. €€€

La Boveda
Carrer Botería 3
Tel: 971 714 863
Great *tapas* bar, full of life, known for the best *pa amb oli* in Palma. Also does full meals. Be prepared to queue. Stays open late as a (drinking) bar. There's another branch, with more modern décor, at *Passeig Sagrera 3, tel: 971 720 026*. Both closed Sun. €

Above: lunch is a leisurely affair
Right: sangria

Porto Pi
Avinguda Joan Miró 174
Tel: 971 400 087
One of Mallorca's best-known restaurants. Good food in a lovely manor house. Michelin star. Closed Sun and Sat lunch. €€€

Around the Island
Algaida
Cal Dimoni
Carretera Palma–Manacor Km21
Tel: 971 665 035
Sobrasadas hang from the ceiling waiting to be cooked over an open fire. €

Es 4 Vents
Carretera Palma–Manacor Km21
Tel: 971 665 173
Popular venue for large family Sunday lunches. Closed Thur. €–€€

Bunyola
Ses Porxeres
Carretera Palma–Sóller Km17
Tel: 971 613 762
Catalan cuisine. Game specialities recommended. Reservations essential. €€€

Cala Ratjada
Ses Rotjes
Carrer Rafael Blanes 21
Tel: 971 563 108
Michelin-starred restaurant in a hotel of the same name. Excellent fish and meat. €€€

Deià
Ca'n Quet
Hotel Es Molí, Carretera Valldemossa–Deià
Tel: 971 639 196
Superb international food with island influences, served on a terrace with mountain views. Closed Mon. €€€

Jaume
Archiduc Lluis Salvador 24
Tel: 971 639 029
Popular and friendly place prepares generous helpings of authentic Mallorcan food. Dinner only; closed Mon. €€€

Inca
Celler Ca'n Amer
Carrer Pau 39
Tel: 971 501 261
One of the best known of the *cellers*, this family-run establishment also has a huge selection of wines. €€

Celler Can Ripol
Carrer Jaume Armengol 4
Tel: 971 500 024
Another real Mallorcan *celler*, more than 300 years old. Slightly refined local cuisine, reasonable prices and a comprehensive wine list. A real gem. €€

Pollença
Clivia
Avinguda Pollentia 7
Tel: 971 533 635/971 534 616
An elegant, lace-curtained setting in which to enjoy Mallorcan cuisine; baked sea bass and mountain ham are two favourites. Closed Tues lunch. €€

Stay
Moll Nou s/n, Port de Pollença
Tel: 971 864 013
A smart restaurant in the centre of the port that has been operating for years. Mainly fish, but meat also features and is well presented. €€–€€€

Trencadora
Carrer Ramon Llull 7
Tel: 971 531 859
Eat on the terrace, in a courtyard garden or indoors. Organic products used whenever possible. Good value set menus. €€

Port d'Andratx
Miramar
Avinguda Mateo Bosch 22
Tel: 971 671 617
Long-established and fashionable restaurant at the water's edge, with good seafood. €€€

Randa
Es Recó de Randa
Carrer Font 13
Tel: 971 660 997
Local and international cuisine are served at this welcoming restaurant, attached to an excellent small hotel. Specialises in suckling pig *(lechona)*. Outdoor terrace. €€€

Sineu
Celler de Ca'n Font
Sa Plaça s/n
Tel: 971 520 313/295
Another excellent, traditional *celler*, in a hotel of the same name. *Sopas mallorquinas*, roast suckling pig *(lechona)* and rice dishes are the specialities. €€

eating out

NIGHTLIFE

Life in Mallorca is as varied late at night as it is at noon. In the words of Santiago Rusiñol, the Mallorcans 'take the moon' as others 'take the sun'. Theatrical performances and concerts usually begin at 10pm. Cinemas have after-midnight *ciclos* which attract large crowds. Cafés and bars are hopping until way past midnight. And no one would dream of arriving at a restaurant for dinner before 9.30 or 10pm. In fact, Mallorcans – urban ones, at least – are dedicated to almost any activity which keeps them from going home too early.

In the large resorts, especially those in the south of the island, clubs and discos keep going all night, catering mainly to a very young tourist crowd. They come and go with great rapidity and predicting next season's hot spot would be unwise. However, there is no shortage of leaflets and posters and special offers to lure customers in and the decibel level is often so high that they would be hard to miss. BCM in Magaluf, with laser shows and top DJs, is the biggest disco on the island.

Cafés and Bars

Pub crawls, which may better be termed café crawls, are the most common activity in Palma. Mallorcan summer evenings are made for sitting on a terrace, sipping a beer or *café con hielo* and enjoying a *tertulia* (chat) until your eyelids are fighting to stay open. In Palma, the traditional cafés such as **Café Lírico** in Plaça de la Reina or **Bar Bosch**, not far away in Plaça Rei Joan Carles I, **Café La Llotja**, opposite the eponymous building, and **La Bóveda** nearby at Carrer Boteria 3, fill up around 10pm and stay full until their doors close at two or three in the morning. Alternatively, indulge yourself with a cocktail at the **Abaco**, Carrer Sant Joan 1 – a wonderfully over-the-top bar in a former palace, with exotic décor, caged birds and operatic background music. Very kitsch, not cheap, but good fun.

As Mallorca modernises, so does its nightlife. Today's *tertulias*, as often as not, take place in chic waterfront cafés in smart **Porto Portals** where you may catch a glimpse of members of the international glitterati sitting at nearby tables.

Clubs and Discos

The narrow streets around SaLlotja in Palma, are home to a number of late-night bars, while the more upmarket bars and clubs are a little further out of town, mostly clustered around Avinguda Gabriel Roca, the western end of the Passeig Marítim, described as 'the nerve centre of Palma's nightlife'. The Santa Catalina district is also up-and-coming.

The **Club de Mar**, at the marina, is a smart place, popular with the yachting crowd and Palma's rich and famous; *the* place to go here is the **Mar Salada**, Muelle Pelaires s/n. The **Garito Café** at Darsena Ca'n Barbará at the end of Passeig Marítim is currently one of the coolest spots in town, as is the **Minimal Bar** on Passeig Mallorca. The long-established **Tito's** at Avinguda Gabriel Roca 33, with its exterior glass lift, has loud music and a laser light show. Just down the road at No 42, a younger crowd lines up for hours to get into **Pachá**, with inside and outside bars and top DJs. Such places rarely get going until after midnight.

Meanwhile, the older set go dancing at the **Victoria Boite** (at the Hotel Victoria, again on Gabriel Roca) or meet for drinks at one of the many piano bars, such as **Romance** (Carrer Marqués de la Cenia 37).

For Latin sounds, the well-known **Made in Brasil** at Avinguda Gabriel Roca 27, is your best bet and has its own dance classes (tel: 971 372 390) so you can learn to lambada and samba in style.

Café Barcelona Jazz Club at Carrer Apuntadors 5 is a long-established place with live jazz and blues; and its newer neighbour, **Golden Door**, at No. 3 is a chic little spot. **Spirits**, Carrer Jaume Ferrer 18, with a dance floor, is smart and relatively new, and is gaining a loyal following.

Flamenco

Flamenco isn't big in Mallorca, as it has little to do with the island culture, but you can sometimes catch performances at **La Caseta Rociera**, on the Passeig Marítim in Palma. **Al Andalus** at Carrer Gavina 7 in Cala Major is another place to try.

Theatre and Music

The island hosts myriad other music possibilities, from classical guitar competitions and jazz festivals to piano recitals. There are splendid festivals of classical music in Deià, Pollença, Valldemossa and Artà in July and August and organ recitals in many of the island's churches. In summer, it seems that life on Mallorca becomes one long concert *(see Calendar of Special Events)*. In the winter months, the tourist board promotes classical concerts, which take place in historic locations all over the island.

L'Auditorio, at Passeig Marítim 18 has two acoustically excellent concert halls, the Sala Magna and the Sala Mozart, which stage classical concerts as well as theatre, opera, ballet and comedy (tel: 971 735 328, bookings: tel: 902 332 211, www.auditorium-pm.com). The Ciutat de Palma Symphony Orchestra has its home here. Concerts are also held in the **Centro Cultural de la**

Misericòrdia in Via Roma, tel: 971 713 346 and, in summer, in the delightful music room of the **Palau March**, tel: 971 711 122, www.fundbmarch.es. The grand Teatre Principal in Plaça Weyler is currently closed for extensive renovation work, but the **Teatre Municipal**, Passeig de Mallorca 9, tel: 971 739 148, stages contemporary drama, dance and films. Free outdoor concerts – jazz, rock and classical – are held in the beautiful setting of the **Parc de la Mar** below the city walls on some summer evenings. A bar serves drinks and snacks and there's a cheerful party atmosphere.

Dinner and Spectacle

A phenomenon which arrived with the tourists a few decades ago is the 'dinner and spectacle' evening. That they're still going strong is the best indication of their popularity. If you are staying in one of the hotels where they are staged, you will soon find out about them; and if you are staying nearby, there will be local publicity about the events. Otherwise, contact the municipal tourist office for details.

Mallorca's only **Casino** is at Urbanización Sol de Mallorca, Magaluf, Calvià, tel: 971 130 000 (open till 5am). Dress is casual but you need to take your passport.

Above: outdoor dining at Cala d'Or

SPORTS & ACTIVITIES

Golf

Mallorca is home to a dozen excellent golf courses, in beautiful natural settings. The island also hosts several international competitions each year. A few courses are:

Real Golf de Bendinat: 18 hole, par 68; 8km (5 miles) from Palma on the road to Andratx. Tel: 971 405 200.

Golf Pollença: 9 hole, par 72; 50km (31 miles) from Palma, 2km (1½ miles) from Pollença. Challenging course in a beautiful setting. Tel: 971 533 216.

Golf Santa Ponça I: 18 hole, par 72; 18km (12 miles) from Palma. One of the longest courses in Europe. Tel: 971 690 211.

Son Vida Golf: 18 hole, par 72; on the outskirts of Palma in the Son Vida development. The oldest course on the island, with great views over Palma bay. Tel: 971 791 210. Hosts the Balearics Open.

Vall D'Or Golf Club: men's professional and women's amateur tees; 18 hole, par 71; 60km (37 miles) from Palma, between Porto Colom and Cala D'Or. Attractive course with sea views. Tel: 971 837 001.

For further information contact the Federació Balear de Golf, Avinguda Jaume III 17, Palma, tel: 971 722 753.

Water Sports

Sailing, windsurfing, water-skiing and scuba diving are all popular activities. The island is a major sailing centre, with well-equipped marinas catering for all kinds of vessels, including those of the mega rich. For sailing lessons, the **Escuela Nacional de Vela Calanova**, Avinguda Joan Miró 327, Palma, tel: 971 402 512, offers intensive beginners' courses and general advice, as does the **Centro Náutico Port de Sóller**, Platja d'En Repic, Port de Sóller, tel: 971 633 001, www.nauticsoller.com. **Sail and Surf Pollença**, Passeig Saralegui, Port de Pollença, tel: 971 865 346, is also recommended.

Windsurfing, **water-skiing** and **scuba diving** are possible at most resorts. **Centro Náutico Port de Sóller** and **Sail and Surf Pollenç**a (*see above*) both offer windsurf hire and tuition, as does **Llaüts**, Camino San Carlos 6A, Port d'Andratx, tel: 971 672 094. The **Ski Club Calanova**, Carrer Condor 22, Son Ferrer, Santa Ponça, tel: 971 100 328 is also recommended. In the southwest there are **scuba diving** centres at Sant Elm (**Scuba Activa**, tel: 971 239 102), and Port d'Andratx (**Aqua Marine Diving**, tel: 971 674 376); in the northeast at Cala Ratjada (**Mero Diving**, tel: 971 565 467).

Above: windsurfing at Port d'Alcúdia

Hiking, Climbing and More

The Mallorcan landscape is great for **hiking** and **climbing**. Some routes are challenging – especially those in the Tramuntana region – others more gentle. Local tourist offices have details of the walking routes in their vicinity. The **Grup Excursionista de Mallorca**, Carrer Andreu Feliu 20, Palma, tel: 971 947 900 www.gemweb.org has good information for climbers; as does **Rocaroja**, Plaça del Mercat 15, Palma, tel: 616 754 679, www.rocaroja.com. The **Parc Natural de Mondragó**, tel: 971 181 022 offers walking trails through pine groves, dunes and marshland in the southeast of the island.

The sunny climate, beautiful scenery and a network of quiet back-roads make Mallorca ideal for **cycling**. There are bike hire companies in all the resorts and larger towns around the island, and most will have mountain bikes as well as standard ones.

Horse riding is popular, with facilities in many of the tourist areas. Contact the **Escuela de Equitación de Mallorca**, Carretera Sóller Km 12, tel: 971 613 157 for more information. Bird watching is popular, too. Numerous migrating birds stop off here in spring. the **Parc Natural de S'Albufera**, tel: 971 892 250 has the widest variety and the **Parc Natural de Mondragó**, tel: 971 181 022 is a rewarding site for spotting marine birds.

Amusement/Theme Parks

Mallorca is a popular destination for family holidays and has a wide variety of attractions to cater for all ages, with water parks a perennial favourite.

Acuario de Mallorca

Porto Cristo (150m/yds from the Coves del Drach, tel: 971 820 971. Large aquarium complex.

Aquacity

Palma–Arenal motorway, Exit 5, tel: 971 440 000, www.aspro.ocio.com. Huge water park with slides, etc.

Aquapark

Carretera Cala Figuera, Magaluf, tel: 971 130 811, www.aspro.ocio.com. Water park with a Boomerang slide.

Hidropark

Avinguda Tucán s/n, Port d'Alcúdia. Tel: 971 891 672. Water park with mini-golf.

Magaluf Karting

Carretera Cala Figuera, Magaluf, tel: 971 131 134. Next to Aquapark, caters to older children and teenagers.

Marineland

Costa d'en Blanes, Palma–Andratx motorway, Portals Nous exit, tel: 971 675 125. Dolphins, sea lions, parrots and a reptile house, plus gardens and beach.

Natura Park Santa Eugènia

Carretera de Sineu, Km 15. Tel: 971 144 078. Animals and birds of prey.

Nemo Submarine

Magaluf, tel: 971 130 244. Expensive but popular 50-minute submarine trips. Departures Mar–Oct daily 9am–5pm on the hour.

Safari-Zoo

Sa Coma, Carretera Porto Cristo–Cala Millor. Tel: 971 810 909. Safari park; tour by mini-train or in your own car.

Right: taking a dip

CALENDAR OF EVENTS

Mallorca is a cultural centre *par excellence*. Most towns and villages have a local festival, usually celebrating their patron saint but sometimes, as in the case of the Christians and Moors festival in Sóller, in honour of a particular historical event. Many of these festivals are genuinely worth seeing. They happily mix the sacred with the secular, and usually incorporate dancing, eating and drinking, and many of them include appearances by *cavallets* – dancers with cardboard hobby-horses strapped to them – and *dimoni* – red-clad devils. There are also a number of prestigious musical events in Mallorca in summer, which are held in beautiful surroundings and attract some of the world's finest musicians. It is wise to book for these events if you can, but it is often possible to get a ticket on the night.

In the following list, music and cultural festivals that take place throughout most of a given month have been listed first, followed by festivals on specific dates.

The tourist office publishes details of major events and there is usually plenty of local advertising.

January

5–6: Reis Mags (Three Kings). A colourful procession to celebrate Epiphany, which is as important as Christmas. **Palma**.

16–17: Sant Antoni Abat. Bonfires, dancing and traditional eel pies *(espinagades)* on 16th; on the following day domestic and farm animals are paraded through the streets to receive a blessing from the patron saint of pets. This is now the only day when the church of Sant Antoniet in Palma is used for religious services. **Palma, Sa Pobla, Artà and other towns**.

19–20: Festa de Sant Sebastià. Festival of the saint, staged in different squares around the towns, with dances by *cavallets*. **Palma, Pollença**.

February

pre-Lent, dates vary: Carnival. Celebrated with fancy dress parades and general revelry. **Palma and other towns throughout the island**.

March–April

Easter celebrations, dates vary: Fira del Ram (Palm Festival) on Palm Sunday. **Semana Santa** (Holy Week) is celebrated in **Palma** and throughout the island with solemn processions. In **Pollença** the **Devallament** (Lowering) sees a figure of Christ brought down from the Oratori on the hill on Good Friday. There are also pilgrimages *(romerias)* to the many hilltop sanctuaries around the island, including the Romeria al Castell de Alaró in **Alaró**.

5 April: Local fiesta. **Cala de Sant Vicenç**.
23: Sant Jordi (St George's Day). **Most parts of the island**.

May

late May–early June: Fira del Llibre (Book Fair). **Palma**.
8–10: Cristians i Morus (also called **Ses Valentes Dones** – the Valiant Women). Mock battles between Moors and Christians commemorating an occasion in 1561 when local women joined in the fight against Turkish pirates. **Sóller**.

June

13: Sant Antoni de Padua. Festival incorporating *dimoni* and *cavallets*. **Artà**.

Left: Easter parade

Thursday after Trinity Sunday, the ninth after Easter: Corpus Christi processions. **Pollença**.
24: Festival of Sant Joan. Midsummer street parties, dancing, bonfires, etc. **Muro, Sant Joan, Formentor.**

July

Music Festival of Artà. Classical music performed on Sundays throughout July and into the first week of August. Tel: 971 835 017, www.alcudia.net.
Pollença Festival of Classical Music. July and August in the cloister of Sant Domingo. Festival established in 1962. International artists perform in a beautiful setting. Tel: 971 535 077, www.festivalpollenca.org.
Deià Festival. Chamber music in July and August performed both in the tiny parish church and in the stunning setting of nearby Son Marroig. Tel: 971 639 178, www.sound-post.org.
Serenates d'Estiu (Summer Serenades). July and August, various buildings in **Capdepera** and **Cala Ratjad**a. Tel: 971 563 033.
Serenates d'Estiu. Weekly classical music performances in July and August in Bellver Castle, **Palma**. Tel: 971 728 841.
Mediterranean Folk Groups. In Parc de la Mar, **Palma**. Tel: 971 711 527.
Gospel Choral Concert. Mid-July. **Torrent de Pareis**. Tel: 971 725 210.
Sa Mostra. Late July. International folklore festival with participants from all over the world. **Sóller**. www.samostra.org.
2: Romeria de la Victòria. **Alcúdia**.
16: Festes de la Verge del Carmen; colourful land and sea processions in honour of the saint of seafarers and fishermen. **Port d'Andratx, Cala Ratjada, Port de Sóller, Port de Pollença**.
last Sunday: Festes de Sant Jaume.A major religious and secular festival in **Alcúdia**. **Calvià, Muro, Santanyí and other towns** also celebrate.
27–28: Festes de Santa Catalina Tomàs, Mallorca's saint is honoured in her home town. **Valldemossa**.

August

Concerts on the Grass. Classical music in the open air, every Saturday. **Golf Club of Bendinat**. Tel: 971 405 200.
Frédéric Chopin Festival. Classical music performed in La Real Cartuja, **Valldemossa**. Tel: 971 612 351, www.festivalchopin.com.
International Music Festival of Cura. Weekly concerts. Tel: 971 205 026.
International Jazz Festival, Sa Pobla. Tel: 972 542 530.
2: Festa de Nostra Señora dels Angels – 'Es Firó'. **Pollença**.
24: Festes de Sant Bartomeu. The saint's day is celebrated with *cavallets* (hobby-horse dancers). **Montuíri, Capdepera**.
28: Festa de Sant Agustí. With *cavallets*. **Felanitx**.

September

First Sunday: Processió de la Beata. **Santa Margalida**.
20–1: Festa de Sant Mateu. **Bunyola**.
Last Sunday: Festa des Vermar (Wine Festival). **Binissalem**.

October

First Sunday: Torrada des Botifarró. A very local celebration that centres on eating regional sausages and vegetable pies, and folk dancing. **Sant Joan**.
Third Saturday: Fiesta de La Beata. A festival honouring Santa Catalina Tomàs. Decorated floats from all over the island join a procession. **Palma**.

November

late November: Saint Cecilia, patron saint of music, is celebrated with a week of concerts and cultural tours. **Palma**.
Dijous Bó. Street market and craft fair. **Inca**.
30: Festa de Sant Andreu. **Santanyí**:

December

31: Festa de l'Estàndard. Commemorates the Christian reconquest of the island in 1229. Procession from the Town Hall to the Cathedral. **Palma**.

Practical Information

GETTING THERE

By Air
Palma de Mallorca's huge Son Sant Joan airport is linked by regular scheduled non-stop flights from London, Dublin, Berlin and Frankfurt, with frequent flights from many other European cities. Flights from the US and Canada also go via London airports and Barcelona or Madrid. For scheduled flights from the UK, contact Iberia, the Spanish national carrier, tel: 0845 850 9000, <www.iberia.com> or British Airways, tel: 0845 773 3377, <www.ba.com>.

In the US contact Iberia, tel: 1-800 772 4642, <www.iberia.com/ibusa>; Continental Airlines, tel: 1-800 231 0856, <www.flycontinental.com>.

Numerous budget airlines fly to Palma from airports all over the UK. Booking via the Internet is usually the cheapest method for flight-only tickets. All-inclusive package deals are the cheapest way to holiday in Mallorca.

The airport is situated about 11km (7 miles) from the city centre. There are buses every 20 minutes (journey time about 30 minutes). Taxis are readily available (journey time about 15–20 minutes) and fares are reasonable.

By Boat
Car ferries operate daily from Barcelona and Valencia to Palma. The slower, overnight trip takes 8 hours on Trasmediterránea (Moll de Paraires, Estació Marítim 2, tel: 902 454 645 or 971 702 300/971 366 050 in Palma; <www.trasmediterranea.com>); during peak holiday season, it also operates a faster ferry, which takes 4½ hours. Baleària operates a fast ferry from Barcelona to Alcúdia on Saturday and Sunday, which takes 3½ hours (tel: 902 160 180, <www.balearia.net>), and a slower one via Menorca on weekdays (5½ hours). Faster still is the Buquebus (Moll de Paraires, Estació Marítim 3, tel: 934 817 360 in Barcelona or 971 400 969 in Palma; e-mail <reserves@buquebus.es>) (3 hours).

TRAVEL ESSENTIALS

Visas and Passports
British citizens just need a valid passport to enter Mallorca or any part of Spain. Visitors from other EU countries require a valid National Identity Card from their home country, as do citizens of Andorra, Austria, Liechtenstein, Monaco and Switzerland. US citizens, Australians and New Zealanders just require a valid passport and are automatically authorised for a three-month stay, which can be renewed for another three months. Visitors from other countries should check with the Spanish Consulate in their own country.

Electricity
Mallorca has converted to 220 volts AC. British 240-volt appliances work perfectly well but will need an adaptor as sockets are the two round pin type.

Left: the Orange Express tram
Right: an even slower mode of transport

Climate

Mallorca enjoys a Mediterranean climate. From mid-June until September the island is virtually rainless, with wall-to-wall sunshine. Temperatures in the hottest month, July, range from around 30°C (86°F) in the afternoon (rather high for walking and sightseeing), to about 20°C (68°F) at night. Hotels and taxis are usually air-conditioned.

There are often short, heavy rains in early September. Autumn sees pleasant temperatures (typically around 24°C (75°F) and sun, although there is some rain – October is statistically the wettest month of the year.

In winter, the weather is a little uncertain, with some rain and cool winds, although most days are sunny and it is usually warm enough at midday to sit outside at a café. Average max/min temperatures are 15°C (59°F) and 7°C (45°F). April and May see a little rain but lots of sunshine and moderate temperatures.

When to Visit

Summer is the traditional time to visit Mallorca but the high season implies crowded beaches, hot, sticky days and queues at the most popular places. The island government is trying to promote off-season tourism, which makes sense. A good time to go is in mid-autumn, when the sky is a deep blue and the low season prices have begun. The nights are cool enough for a jacket, but the days are still pleasantly warm. A still better option is early spring, a beautiful time, just after the end of the winter rains. From late January onwards the wildflowers begin to carpet the fields, and the almond blossom appears in the countryside in February.

Above: working on the suntan
Right: bar life, Pollença

Local Time

Mallorca is 2 hours ahead of GMT in the summer and 1 hour ahead in the winter.

MONEY MATTERS

The euro has been the Spanish monetary unit since 2002. Bank notes are available in denominations of 5, 10, 20, 50, 100, 200 and 500 euros, and there are coins for 1 and 2 euros and for 1, 2, 5, 10, 20 and 50 cents

Banks offer the best rates and charge no commission. Many travel agencies exchange foreign currency, and *casas de cambio* stay open outside banking hours.

Major international credit cards are widely recognised, but smaller businesses tend to prefer cash. Visa/Eurocard/Master-Card are the most generally accepted. Credit and debit cards are also useful for obtaining cash from ATMs – cash machines – which are found in all towns and resorts. They offer the most convenient way of obtaining cash and usually the best exchange rate.

Many hotels, shops, restaurants and travel agencies cash travellers' cheques, and so do banks, where you're likely to get a better rate (you will need your passport).

Banks open Monday–Friday 9am–2pm, and Saturday 9am–1pm (in winter). Savings banks sometimes have longer hours.

Tipping

The usual tip is 10 percent. In some restaurants service is already included (look for *servicio incluído* on the bill). It is also usual to tip taxi drivers, hairdressers, etc.

GETTING ACQUAINTED

How Not to Offend

As a rule, Mallorcans are fairly easy-going people. Be respectful of their religion: even though the majority of the population doesn't go to Mass on a regular basis, Mallorcans will jump on an outside detractor if Catholicism is belittled in any way.

practical information

Clothing

To avoid causing offence remember that, anywhere except on beaches, a T-shirt and shorts is the minimum requirement for both men and women. Never wear beach gear in towns. When visiting churches you should also cover your shoulders and knees. Although a great percentage of the younger population is happy to walk the island's beaches topless, total nudity should be kept to specifically designated beaches (and there aren't many of them). A little common sense goes a long way.

Whom do you Trust?

As far as avoiding crime is concerned, you should employ the same precautions as you would at home. Remember to keep your eye on your purse and camera at all times, especially in crowded areas such as markets and busy tourist sites, and take care when withdrawing money from ATMs. Leave valuables in the hotel safe; make a photocopy of your passport and carry that with you, leaving the original in the safe. If you hired a car, don't leave your property visible inside.

You are advised to check your change in tourist areas. If you feel you've been 'had' in a bar, check the prices against the list posted on the wall. If there is no list, the owner is already in violation of the law and you can ask for the *Libro de Reclamaciones* (Complaints Book) and fill out a complaint (the language isn't important but put your passport number and name with it). This isn't the waste of time it might seem. The pages are all numbered and are checked by inspectors every few months. If a page is missing, the owner is in trouble. If there is a complaint, he is obliged to answer for it or pay a fine or lose his licence. Because this is a very serious matter for the owner, you should be as objective as possible about the misdemeanor.

As the number of foreigners interested in buying houses increases, so does the number of lawyers hoping to take advantage of them. The property trade here is a complicated business and requires the same legal attention it does in any country. Listen to the experiences of your fellow countrymen but don't take them as legal advice. There are lots of reputable English-speaking Spanish lawyers around who are willing to help. Your embassy can supply a list of names.

TOURIST INFORMATION

Tourist information is readily available in most parts of Mallorca, although many information offices close in winter. The following list is not comprehensive.

Local Tourist Offices

Palma: Plaça de la Reina 2, tel: 971 712 216, fax: 971 720 251; Carrer Constitució 1, tel: 971 725 396; Plaça d'Espanya, tel: 971 754 329; Carrer Sant Domingo 11, tel: 971 724 090, fax: 971 720 240 (municipal office – information on Palma only).

Airport. Tel/fax: 971 789 556.

Cala Ratjada: Plaça des Pins, tel: 971 563 033; fax: 971 565 256.

Colònia Sant Jordi: Dr Barraquer, tel: 971 656 073, fax: 971 656 447 (closed Nov–Mar).

Pollença: Carrer Sant Domingo, tel: 971 535 077, fax: 971 866 746.

Port d'Alcúdia: Carrer Mariners s/n, tel: 971 547 257, fax: 971 892 615 (closed Nov–Mar).

Port de Pollença: Carrer Joan XXIII 46, tel: 971 865 467, fax: 971 866 746.

Port de Sóller: Canonge Oliver 10, tel: 971 633 042 (closed Nov–Mar).

Porto Colom: Avinguda Cala Marsal, tel: 971 825 768.

Sóller: Plaça de la Constitució, tel: 971 630 200, fax: 971 633 722.

Valldemossa: Avinguda Arxiduc Lluis Salvador, tel/fax: 971 612 106 (closed Nov–Mar).

Spanish Tourist Offices Abroad

Canada: 2 Bloor St W, Suite 3402, Toronto, Ontario M4W 3E2, tel: (416) 961 31 31, www.tourspaintoronto.on.ca.

United Kingdom:79 New Cavendish Street, London W1W 6XB, tel: (020) 7486 8077, fax: (020) 7486 8034, brochure line: tel: 09063 640 630, www.tourspain.co.uk.
Please note that this office is only open to personal callers by appointment.

USA: 666 Fifth Avenue, New York, NY 10103, tel: (212) 265 8822, fax: (212) 265 8864, www.okspain.org; 8383 Wilshire Blvd, Suite 956, Beverly Hills, CA 90211, tel: (323) 658 7188, fax: (323) 658 1061; 1221 Brick-ell Avenue, Miami FL 33131, tel: (305) 358 1992.

Above: the Mallorcan flag
Right: hairpin bends on the Formentor Peninsula

GETTING AROUND

Driving in Mallorca

Most foreign driving licences are accepted in Mallorca. Seatbelts are compulsory for front and back seats. Roads are generally in good condition, although many are narrow and mountain routes have numerous hair-pin bends and can get very busy in the sum-mer. If you wish to stop to admire the view, make sure you find somewhere sensible to pull over. The motorway that loops around to the north of Palma (connecting the air-port with points west of the city), is known as the *Via Cintura* and is signposted as such.

Parking can be difficult. In Palma your best bet is to head for one of the city centre underground car parks (for instance at the Plaça Mayor or opposite the cathedral at the Parc de la Mar). Parking fines are steep, and as it is more difficult to collect fines from tourists, there is a tendency to tow away hire cars first.

Hiring cars is inexpensive, and all of the major international agencies are represented. Cars may be hired at the airport or through a travel agent in town. In high season it is often the case that the local rental companies will not consider renting for periods of fewer than three or four days. You can get some good deals by booking a car in advance on the internet, although some companies will only arrange pick-ups at the aiport. Always check what's included in the price: third-party insurance is, by law, but fully com-prehensive is usually extra.

It is possible to hire a wide range of vehi-cles, and almost all will have air-condition-ing. Even if you have a four-wheel drive, we suggest you stick to the roads and leave nature to the hikers.

Taxis

Palma has several taxi ranks, or cabs can be hailed on the street. Taxis in and around Palma are cheap compared to other Euro-pean locations, and have meters. Extra charges are normal for items of luggage and trips to and from the airport. Trips across the island, however, are quite expensive. The official prices are posted at all cab ranks, and drivers also carry a list. Taxis can usually be ordered at hotel reception desks.

Buses

There are several bus companies in Mallorca, travelling to virtually every point on the island. In Palma, most services begin their journeys at the Plaça d'Espanya or the new bus station close by in Carrer Eusebio Estada (near the railway station). City buses are also efficient. There is a set fare for city journeys and you buy your ticket on the bus. A Palma bus schedule (from Empresa Municipal de Transports, EMT) detailing city routes is available from the tourist office. Bus services are reduced on Sunday and holidays. Fewer services run during the winter months.

In Palma it is worth buying a 10-trip *bono* booklet of tickets, available from tobacconists' shops or kiosks. There is no time limit on these tickets.

Trains

As well as the famous old train, dating from 1912, which runs six times a day (seven on Sunday) between **Palma** and **Sóller**, there is a train from Palma's **Plaça d'Espanya** to **Inca**. This now runs on to Llubi, Muro and Sa Pobla. Primarily a commuter train, it leaves both the island capital and Inca about once every hour, with extra trains at rush hours, stopping at **Santa María**, **Consell** and **Binissalem** along the way. For Sóller trains,

tel: 971 752 051; for Inca trains, tel: 971 752 245, or ask at the station.

Trams

The old tram (known as the Orange Express) that connects Sóller and Port de Sóller runs every half-hour from 7am to 8.15pm. It is a rattling, scenic, 20-minute journey, with stops on route where requested.

Boat

There are dozens of boat excursions operating in summer (weather permitting). Some of the most popular are those to the islands of Sa Dragonera (from Sant Elm) and Cabrera (from Colónia de Sant Jordi). **Creuer-Sóller**, Muelle Comercial s/n, Port de Sóller, tel: 689 686 834 and its associate companies **Tramontana SA**, tel: 971 633 109, and **Barcos Azules**, tel: 971 630 170, run a variety of trips around the rugged northwest coast and tiny bays, including Cap Formentor and Sa Calobra. The glass-bottomed **Dolphin D'Or**, tel: 971 657 012, runs from Porto Colom. All are listed in the pamphlet *Excursiones en Barca*, available from tourist offices, and posters and flyers in the ports advertise trips.

Horse Carts

At various sites in Palma there are ranks of horse drawn *galeras* waiting to whisk you off on a romantic tour of the old city. The prices are fixed and the tour of the old city takes about an hour.

WHERE TO STAY

The following guide indicates prices for a double room in high season, but should be used as an approximate guide only. VAT (IVA) at 7 percent and breakfast are sometimes included in a hotel's quoted rate, sometimes not, so it is wise to check.

€€€€ = over €240
€€€ =€120–240)
€€ =€60–120
€ = below €60

Hotels in Palma

Almudaina
Avinguda Jaume III 9
Tel: 971 727 340
Fax: 971 722 599
Comfortable, moderately priced, with obliging staff, right in the centre of town. €€

Bellver
Avinguda Gabriel Roca 11
Tel: 971 735 142
Comfortable hotel west of the city centre. Sea views, pleasant garden, swimming pool, restaurant and cafeteria. €€€€

Born
Carrer Sant Jaume 3
Tel: 971 712 942
Fax: 971 718 618
www.hotelborn.com
Tastefully renovated palace, right in the city centre. Breakfast is served in the cafeteria or on the lovely patio. A real gem. €€

Convent de la Missió
Carrer de la Missió 7
Tel: 971 227 347
www.conventdelamissio.com
Opened in 2003 in a 17th-century convent in the old town. Light, airy rooms, roof terrace and recommended restaurant. €€€

Dalt Murada
Carrer Almudaina 6
Tel: 971 425 300
Fax: 971 719 708
www.hoteldaltmurada.com
Attractive and friendly little hotel in a restored manor house near the cathedral. Reservations recommended. €€

Palacio Ca Sa Galesa
Carrer Miramar 8
Tel: 971 715 400
Fax: 971 721 579
www.palaciosagalesa.com
Small exclusive hotel in a restored *palacio* in the heart of medieval Palma. Wonderful views of the cathedral and Palma Bay from the roof terrace. €€€€

Puro
Carrer Montenegro 12
Tel: 971 425 450
www.purohotel.com
Designer chic in a converted palace, with a lively bar and restaurant – the Opio. €€€

Saratoga
Passeig Mallorca 6
Tel: 971 727 240
Great location close to the heart of the city, with spacious rooms and comprehensive facilities. €€€€

San Lorenzo
Carrer Sant Llorenç (San Lorenzo) 14
Tel: 971 728 200
Fax: 971 711 901
www.hotelsanlorenzo.com
Only six rooms, in a lovingly restored 17th-century mansion in old Palma, with attractive gardens. Reservations essential. €€€

Tres
Carrer Apuntadors 3
Tel: 971 717 333
www.hoteltres.com
New, cool and stylish, in another converted palace, with a pretty central courtyard and two roof terraces with splendid views. €€€

Ritzi
Carrer Apuntadors 6
Tel/fax: 971 714 610

Good value in the attractive old part of town west of Passeig de Born. 17 rooms, some with shared bathrooms. €

Around the Island

Hotel Formentor
Platja de Formentor s/n
Tel: 971 899 100
Fax: 971 865 155
www.hotelformentor.net
Overlooking the beach, this classic hotel is luxurious and family-run. Surrounded by pine trees and lush gardens. €€€€

Ca n'Ai Hotel Rural
Camí Son Sales 50, Sóller
Tel: 971 632 494
Fax: 971 631 899
www.canai.com
A lovely old manor set among orange groves in the Sóller valley. Outdoor pool. Suites only. Closed Nov–Jan. €€€

Es Molí
Carretera Valldemossa–Deià s/n
Tel: 971 639 090
Fax: 971 639 333
www.esmoli.com
At the foot of Es Teix mountain overlooking Deià and the sea, Es Molí is one of Mallorca's most spectacular hotels. Closed Nov–mid-Apr. €€€€

Bon Sol
Passeig de Illetes, 30
Tel: 971 402 111
Fax: 971 402 559
Beautiful location with a sub-tropical garden, handy for Palma, yet supremely relaxing. Family-run; antique furnishings. €€€€

Scott's
Plaça de la Església 12, Binissalem
Tel: 971 870 100
Elegant, comfortable hotel in the quiet town of Binissalem, well located for trips to all parts of the island. Excellent breakfasts. Period furniture, pleasant courtyards and ambience. €€€€

Cala Sant Vicenç
Carrer Maressers 2, Cala Sant Vicenç
Tel: 971 530 250
Fax: 971 532 084
www.hotelcala.com
Tucked away in the woods, this luxury hotel has a heated outdoor pool, sauna and lovely gardens. Recommended restaurant, the Cavall Bernat. The beach is a short stroll away. Closed Dec–Jan. €€€€

Juma
Plaça Major 9
Pollença
Tel: 971 535 002
Fax: 971 534 155
www.hoteljuma.com
Small and smart, on the bustling main square. Comfortable, slightly old-fashioned rooms. Closed Nov–Mar. €€

Miramar
Passeig Anglada Camarasa 39
Tel: 971 866 400
Fax: 971 867 211
An attractive, long-established beachfront hotel. Try to get a room with a beach-facing balcony. Closed Nov–Mar. €€

Ses Rotges
Rafael Blanes 21, Cala Ratjada
Tel: 971 563 108
Fax: 971 564 345
www.sesrotges.com

Above: the island has a wide range of characterful hotels

In a lovely old villa a short walk from the beach, with a well-known restaurant. Excellent personal service. Closed mid-Nov–mid-Mar, but open for Christmas. €€€

Mar-i-Vent
Carrer Major 49, Banyalbufar
Tel: 971 618 000
Fax: 971 618 201
www.hotelmarivent.com
Wonderful sea views and a swimming pool.Family-run and very comfortable. Closed Dec–Jan. €€€

Fonda Villa Verde
Carrer Ramón Llull 19, Deià
Tel: 971 639 037
Fax: 971 639 485
In a quiet back streetnear the hilltop church, with a lovely patio and 10 simple rooms. Book ahead. Closed Dec–Feb. €

La Residencia
Son Moragues, Deià
Tel: 971 639 011
Fax: 971 639 370
Chic and elegant, set in two 16th-century manor houses. Lovely pool, tennis courts and an excellent restaurant, El Olivo.€€€€

S'Hotel d'es Puig
Es Puig 4, Deià
Tel: 971 639 409
Fax: 971 639 210

www.hoteldespuig.com
Delightful little place with a small pool and a friendly atmosphere. Closed mid-Nov–Feb. €€

León de Sineu
Carrer dels Bous 129
Tel: 971 520 211
Fax: 971 855 058
Elegant, antique-furnished hotel near the centre of this pretty town. Swimming pool, garden, and good restaurant. €€€

Casa d'Artà
Carrer Rafael Blanes 19
Tel/fax: 971 829 163
Small, family-run hotel in the town centre. Well-furnished with good bathrooms. Solarium and roof terrace. Book in advance. €€

Staying at a Monastery

Many hilltop monasteries offer basic accommodation, with simple rooms and low prices. In high season you need to book well ahead. Ermita de Bonany, tel: 971 561 101. Santuari de Lluc, tel: 971 871 525. Santuari del Puig, tel: 971 184 132. Santuari de Sant Salvador, tel: 971 827 282.

Agroturime and Self-Catering

Self-catering holidays are big business, with a wide range of properties from urban apartments to rambling country *fincas*. **Agroturisme** (rural tourism) offers hotels and self-catering properties, some of them in extremely beautiful surroundings. Contact: Agroturisme Balear, Avinguda Gabriel Alomar i Villalonga 8a, 2º, Palma, tel: 971 721 508, fax: 971 727 317 email: agroturismo@mallorcanet.com for details.

Camping

There are only two official campsites, both in the northeast. **Club San Pedro**, Colonia Sant Pere, Artà, tel: 971 589 023, fax: 971 730 448 (open mid-May–mid Sept). **Sun Club Picafort**, Carretera Can Picafort–Port d'Alcúdia, tel: 971 860 002, fax: 971 717 896 (open all year).

Above: poolside view in Palma

HEALTH AND EMERGENCIES

Emergency Telephone Number

Emergencies (police, fire, ambulance) 112.
Otherwise:
Policía Nacional: 091
Policía Municipal: 092
Guardia Civil (traffic): 062

Medical Problems

Mallorca's tap water is fit to drink, but much off it is high in salinity, although its taste varies drastically from town to town. Most people drink bottled water *con gas* (sparkling) or *sin gas* (still) and you are advised to do the same.

A change of food or water can upet your stomach and anti-diarrhoea pills can come in handy, although a pharmacy *(farmacia)* can give you something for stomach upsets, without a prescription. Hours are 9.30am–1.30pm and 5–8pm, but there is always one in a district open late or all night, and a list of 'duty pharmacies' *(farmacia de guardia)* is posted on the windows.

Too much sun is the other most common cause of problems for visitors. The sun can be very fierce; use a high factor sunscreen, wear a hat and try to avoid the midday sun from May to September. Also remember to drink plenty of water to avoid dehydration. Mosquitoes can be a nuisance at times, so bring some insect repellent.

Medical Facilities

European Union citizens are eligible for free treatment in state-run hospitals. Visitors from the UK should obtain a form E111 from a post office before leaving home. However, it is not accepted everywhere so you should also have private health insurance.

Major hospitals and clinics in Palma include: **Centro Médico**, Edificio Reina Constanza, Passeig Marítim (Porto Pi) 8, tel: 971 707 035/55 (many of the staff speak English). **Hospital de la Creu Roja Espanyola** (Red Cross), Carrer Pons i Gallarça 90, tel: 971 751 445. **Hospital Son Dureta**, Carrer Andrea Doria 55, Palma, tel: 971 175 000; **Hospital General**, Plaça del Hospital 3, Palma, tel: 971 728 484; **Policlínica Miramar**, Camino de la Vileta 30, tel: 971 450 212. A private clinic popular with visitors because the staff speak various languages, is **Clínica Femenía SA**, Carrer Camilo José Cela 20, tel: 971 452 323.

Most towns and villages have first aid stations or doctor's surgeries. Ask for the *Casa de Socorro* or the *Cruz (Creu) Roja*. Many resorts have private medical centres *(centros medicos)* where you pay on the spot for a consultation; staff usually speak some English, German and French. First-aid personnel *(practicantes)* make daily rounds of the larger resort hotels.

There are no **dentists** on permanent call. In case of emergency your hotel should be able to find a reputable local dentist.

Police

Mallorca seems to be awash with policemen. There are three types of police, distinguishable by their uniforms. Those in black and white are the **Policía Nacional**, who are in charge of most things. Their headquarters is in Palma at Carrer Ruíz de Alda 8. The **Policía Municipal** (Local or Metropolitan Police) are responsible for traffic control and other urban problems, and are regarded as being more approachable than the others. The **Guardia Civil** are still dressed in their traditional dark green, but have got rid of the *tricornio* hat which was their most identifiable feature for decades. They now have jurisdiction only in rural areas and are most often seen executing traffic duties along the highways.

Palma also has its Port Police, who are dressed in grey and 'parking control police' in blue. Finally, 'tourist police' are found in resort areas in the summer.

If any of your property is lost or stolen you will have to report it to the police. This must be done within 24 hours if you intend to make a claim on your insurance policy (your hotel will point you to the nearest police station).

COMMUNICATIONS AND NEWS

Postal Service

Palma's **Main Post Office** is at Carrer Constitució 5, tel: 971 721 867 and is open Monday to Friday 9am–2pm, 5–8pm, Saturday 9am–1pm. Here you can send or receive telegrams, as well as buy stamps and send parcels. To send a registered letter the stamps and the certification paper must be bought in the basement and filled out before presenting them at one of the certified windows on the main floor.

Other post offices on the island (all recognisable by a yellow-and-white sign and the words *Correos y Telégrafos*) are only open 9am–2pm.Stamps can also be bought at tobacconists' *(estancos)*, which are easily identifiable by their maroon and yellow *Tabacos* sign over the door. The staff can generally help you with the stamps you need to send postcards and letters home.

A fax can be sent from **Telefon CCC**, Carrer Sant Miquel 42, as well as from some

travel agents (look for fax signs outside); a growing number of stationers also offer this service, as do many hotels.

Telephones

Telephone calls can be made in many bars. Most have either a phone with a meter, which can be used for local calls and paid for afterwards, or a phone that accepts as much money as you want to put in and, in theory, returns unused coins.

You can make direct-dial local and international calls from public telephone booths *(cabinas)* in the street. Most operate with both coins and cards; international telephone credit cards can also be used. Instructions for use are given in several languages in the booths. You can also make calls at public telephone offices called *locutorios*. This is much quieter than making a call on the street, and more convenient, as an attendant will place the call for you, and you pay afterwards.

For calls at pay phones, it's wise to use a phone card *(tarjeta telefónica)*, which can be purchased at any *estanco* (tobacconist's shop), or to use a credit card. To make an international call, dial 00 for an international line plus the country code, plus the phone number, omitting any initial zero. Calls are cheaper after 10pm on weekdays, after 2pm on Saturday, and all day Sunday.

The international code for Spain is 34. To call within Spain, you must always dial the area code (971 for the Balearics), then the number, even when phoning with the same town or locality.

Telephone offices are independent of the post office and are identified by a blue-and-white sign. In Palma, the **central telephone office** is located near the main post office at the corner of Carrer Constitució and the Passeig del Born.

Most UK mobile phones can be used in the Balearics, although both making and receiving calls is expensive. Contact your service provider if you are unsure.

Internet

You can access the net in Palma at numerous places. **La Red Cybercafé**, Carrer Concepció 5 and the Hostal Ritzi, Carrer Apuntadors 6 are a couple of good ones. In the resorts you will see internet access signs all over the place; they come and go, but you are unlikely to have trouble finding one.

News Media

Most UK and German newspapers arrive daily in Palma and the main resorts. The Paris-based *International Herald Tribune* and the European edition of the *Wall Street Journal* are available on the day of publication, and *USA Today* is widely available.

The English-language daily, *Majorca Daily Bulletin*, gives local and British news and entertainment listings. The *Diario de Mallorca* and all the Spanish national newspapers and magazines are available.

The BBC World Service and Voice of America (the latter on shortwave only) can be received on any good radio. The Palma local radio station broadcasts in English 24 hours a day on 103.2 FM.

Most hotels and bars have television, broadcasting in Castilian, Catalan (from Barcelona) and Mallorquí. Satellite dishes are sprouting and most tourist hotels offer multiple channels (German, French, Sky, BBC, CNN, etc.).

USEFUL INFORMATION

Business Hours
In Mallorca the hours still revolve around the long lunchtime *siesta*, but now that Spain has become an integral part of Europe the need to modernise has, in some cases, overcome tradition.

Shops normally open Monday to Saturday from 9am–1pm, then from 4 or 5pm until 8pm, although some smaller ones close on Saturday afternoon. Large supermarkets, shopping malls and some department stores keep more European hours, staying open throughout lunch and often until quite late in the evening. In the major resorts shops also open on Sunday. Prior to Christmas most of the stores, big and small, extend their hours to catch the holiday trade.

Major museums keep similar hours to shops, although the more popular ones are increasingly staying open throughout the day (hours of most important museums are given in the relevant part of the text of this guide).

The main Post Office in Palma also keeps similar hours *(see previous page)* but others open only in the morning.

Banks are only open in the mornings from 9am–2pm, Monday to Friday, but some open on Saturday in winter. Savings banks *(caja*

d'ahorro or *caixa d'estalvis*), usually have slightly longer hours; and exchange offices *(casas de cambio)* keep extended hours.

Government offices and institutions are generally open Monday to Friday 9am–1pm.

Restaurants serve lunch from 1–3.30pm. In the evenings, local people usually eat between 9.30 and 11pm. Places catering for foreigners may function from 7pm, and many serve food throughout the afternoon.

Public Holidays
In Mallorca, holidays may change from year to year. The autonomous political agenda means the Mallorcans ignore some Spanish fiestas in favour of others of more local or regional interest.

As in all Roman Catholic countries, local saints' days may be celebrated as holidays, although only the days of the major saints *(see the list below)* are public holidays throughout the island. For Mallorcans, as for all Spaniards, celebrating their saint's day is considered at least as important as celebrating their birthday.

1 Jan: New Year's Day (Año Nuevo/Any Nou)
6 Jan: Epiphany (Reyes Magos/Reis Mags)
19 March: St Joseph (San José/Sant Josep)
Good Friday (Viernes Santo/Divendres Sant)

Above: ornate door knocker, Palma

1 May: Labour Day (Dia del Trabajo/Tre ball)

ninth Thursday after Easter: Corpus Christi

24 June: St John (San Juan/Sant Joan)

29 June: St Peter and Paul (San Pedro y San Pablo/Sant Pere i Sant Pau)

25 July: St James (Santiago/Sant Jaume)

15 Aug: Day of the Assumption (Asun ción/Assumpció)

12 Oct: Spanish National Day (Dia de la Hispanidad/Hispanitat)

1 Nov: All Saints' (Todos los Santos/Tots Sants)

6 Dec: Constitution Day (Dia de la Constitución/Constitució)

8 Dec: Immaculate Conception (Inmaculada Concepción/Concepció)

Christmas Day (Navidad/Nadal)

THE LANGUAGE

Mallorca's language is Mallorquí, a dialect of Catalan. During the Franco era the teaching and publication of Catalan was effectively banned, and replaced by Spanish (*Castillano*) although people still spoke the language at home. With the arrival of regional autonomy in 1978, Catalan/Mallorquí was enthusiastically re-established, and has become a symbol of Mallorcan identity, although everyone can also speak Spanish. What is more, quite a few of the people working in the tourist industry come from mainland Spain and speak no Mallorquí.

Maps and street signs seem to use Castilian or Catalan at random; thus a map may read *Catedral* for the cathedral, while the street signs may use the Catalan word, *Seu*. Most words are fairly similar, but some (such as *Catedral/Seu* are completely unrelated).There are direction signs all over the island indicating various points of touristic or other interest. These are almost always in Catalan, with pictographs.

The use of 'Can' in Catalan is similar to 'chez' in French (ie 'at the house of').

When it comes to everyday colloqui-

alisms and greetings, the differences become greater and arrive at the point where they are totally impenetrable to those who don't speak the language. Even though there are similarities because they are both Romance languages, Catalan is a distinct language, not a dialect of Castilian.

The linguistic issue remains political, with some people feeling very strongly about it. The rector of the local university is quoted as saying, 'Mallorca is a bilingual island – Catalan and English'.

Throughout this book, we have tried to give the Catalan version of the place name.

Words you will see in this book:

English	Castilian	Catalan
Arch	Arco	Arc
Avenue	Avenida	Avinguda
Baths	Baños	Banys
Bay	Bahia	Badia
Beach	Playa	Platja
Cathedral	Catedral	Seu
City	Ciudad	Ciutat
City Hall	Ayuntamiento	Ajuntament
Caves	Cuevas	Coves
Mountain	Monte	Puig
Mountain range	Sierra	Serra
Museum	Museo	Museu
Palace	Palacio	Palau
Park	Parque	Parc
Promenade	Paseo	Passeig
Quay	Muelle	Moll
Square	Plaza	Plaça
Street	Calle	Carrer
(main street)	Calle Mayor	Carrer Major
Theatre	Teatro	Teatre
Village	Pueblo	Pobla
Welcome	Bienvenido	Benvinguts

Place names and street names

Castilian	Catalan
La Llonja	Sa Llotja
La Granja	Sa Granja
Avenida Jaime III	Avinguda Jaume III
San Elmo	Sant Elm
La Puebla	Sa Pobla
Pueblo Español	Poble Espanyol
San Juan	Sant Joan

Right: pleasure boats at Port de Sóller

FURTHER READING

History and General Background

The New Spaniards: A Portrait of the New Spain by John Hooper (Hutchinson). Excellent overview of post-Franco Spanish society.

The Spanish Civil War by Hugh Thomas (Penguin). Definitive, readable account of the war that divided Spain.

Tuning up at Dawn by Tomàs Graves (Fourth Estate). Robert Graves' son writes about life and music on the island.

Wild Olives by William Graves (Hutchinson). Robert Graves' other son's account of growing up in Deià.

Insiders and Outsiders, Paradise and Reality in Mallorca by Jacqueline Waldren (Berghan Books). A small village gains from foreign investment but retains its culture.

Walking/Climbing/Birdwatching

Holiday Walks in Mallorca by Graham Beech (Sigma). Exactly what it says.

Landscapes of Mallorca by Valerie Crespi-Green (Sunflower Books). Exploring Mallorca by car, public transport and on foot.

Trekking in Spain by Marc Dubin (Lonely Planet). Has a detailed chapter on hikes in the Serra de Tramuntana in Mallorca.

48 Walks in Mallorca by Rolf Goetz (Rother Walking Guides). Detailed walking guide.

Walking in Mallorca by June Parker (Cicerone Press). Describes in detail more than 70 hikes all over the island.

Birdwatching in Mallorca by Ken Stoba (Cicerone). Catalogue of birdlife and sites.

Food

The Taste of a Place: Mallorca by Vicky Bennison (Chakula Press). A mouth-watering introduction to Mallorcan food.

Entrée to Mallorca by Patricia Fenn (Quiller Press). Enthusiastic restaurant guide.

Bread and Oil by Tomàs Graves (Univ. of Wisconsin Press). An insider's look at two of Mallorca's great products.

Travel Accounts

A Winter in Majorca by George Sands (Valldemossa Editions). Sand's scathing account of her brief stay on the island in 1838–9 with Frédéric Chopin (trans. and with comments by Robert Graves).

Jogging Round Majorca by Gordon West (Black Swan). Delightful, whimsical account of a journey in the 1920s.

Fiction

The Bloody Bokhara by George Scott (Eye Level Books) Mallorcan murder mystery, set in Scott's Hotel.

School of the Sun by Ana María Matute (Quartet). Rite-of-passage novel set during the civil war.

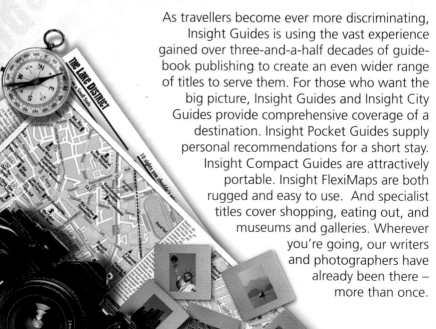

ACKNOWLEDGEMENTS

12, 13(top& bottom), 14, 15, 23, 26, 29 35, 37, 38 (top), 39 (bottom), 39, 44 (top),45, 47,48 (bottom), 68, 76, 79, 82, 86, 94	**Don Murray**
1, 2, 3, 4, 5, 6, 7, 8, 9, 10, 11, 16, 20, 21, 25 (top & bottom), 26 (top& bottom), 27, 31, 32, 34, 36, 38 (bottom), 42, 43, 44 (bottom), 46 (top & bottom), 48 (top), 50, 51, 62, 64 (bottom), 65, 69 (top & bottom), 67 (top & bottom), 70, 71, 72, 74, 75, 77, 80, 81, 84, 85, 87, 88, 89, 91, 92, 95, 97	**Glyn Genin**
28, 53	**Britta Jaschinski**
22, 31	**Tom Le Bas**
13	**Museo de Mallorca**
Back Cover	**Glyn Genin**
Cover	**Pictures Colour Library**
Cartography	**Maria Donnelly**

© APA Publications GmbH & Co. Verlag KG Singapore Branch, Singapore

INDEX